HAPPINESS THAT IS GUARANTEED

BY

GREGORY F. BEARSTOP

© 1998, 2001 by Gregory F. Bearstop. All rights reserved.

No part of this book may be reproduced, stored in a retrieval system, or transmitted by any means, electronic, mechanical, photocopying, recording, or otherwise, without written permission from the author.

ISBN: 0-75965-917-6

This book is printed on acid free paper.

1stBooks – rev. 10/03/01

In loving memory, this book is dedicated to my mother, Gretel Adrian Bearstop.

Acknowledgements

I want to extend a special thanks to my family and friends for their constant support and guidance in this project. Also, I want to specifically thank my two brothers; Andre and Martinez Bearstop; my uncle, William Davis for your assistance; Francis Speltz, who edited this book in the spirit of Christ Himself; and Sheryl Alfei for graciously adding the final touches.

"A gold mine of fresh insights. Bearstop brilliantly sees through the futility of conventional ways of achieving happiness, outlining a new and unique means to personal fulfillment. You won't be the same after reading this book."
>J.D. Miller, CPP-G, MAC
>Author of *Intrinsic Motivation and Psychotherapy*

"Happiness that is Guaranteed is a book to read again and again. With sensitivity and wit, it invites the reader to rethink old and sometimes poisonous notions of happiness and encourages them to press on to true fulfillment."
>Kimberley Lindsay Wilson
>Author of *Work It*

Some of the family members of Mr. Bearstop's clients and others have read the book. Here's what they said:

>"This book grabs your attention."
>
>"It does not promote any particular religion at all; instead, it deals with spirituality, which we all have in common."
>
>"After reading the book, my life has been more fulfilling."
>
>"The book helps you to bring more joy into your life without it being a whole lot of work; this happens as your awareness is heightened by the content."

"It offers believable evidence of an unseen world for which most people yearn."

*Due to confidentiality, the names of the people who commented have been withheld.

TABLE OF CONTENTS

CHAPTER 1
　The Greatest Question 1
CHAPTER 2
　Crisis 21
CHAPTER 3
　Expanding Your Vision of Happiness 34
CHAPTER 4
　Expand Your Vision of Who You Are and What
　You Are Capable of Doing 51
CHAPTER 5
　Expand Your Vision of the Power Within You 62
CHAPTER 6
　What is Blocking You From Your Inner Power? 73
　Food for Thought 79
CHAPTER 7
　Pursuing Your Purpose in Life 94
CHAPTER 8
　Developing Your Relationship with God 107
CHAPTER 9
　A Lasting Relationship with God 136
CHAPTER 10
　The Difference that Developing Your Relationship
　with God Will Make 148

CHAPTER 1

THE GREATEST QUESTION

Are you going through life content, but not really happy? Do you sometimes feel that life has let you down? Could you use more joy in your life?

You may be contending with several problems that are coming at you all at once. You may be getting deeper in debt, you may be struggling in a significant relationship, or you may just feel that your life is not going anywhere. If you want your life to be joyful, exhilarating, and exciting, let me ask you this question: What is the point of your life on this earth? In other words, does your life have any real meaning, or is it true that you are born, struggle through life, die, and that is the end? A contemporary philosopher, Peter Kreeft, in his fascinating book, *Three Philosophies of Life*, says that this question about the meaning of your life is the greatest of all questions. Yet our society doesn't want you to ask this question, because if you did, you might try to answer it and begin to search for the greatest thing, something that would give your life meaning, something that would give you true happiness. And then neither society nor any individual could divert you from true happiness by saying, "Here's money; try that." Society keeps you busy: "Try computers, the Internet, Nintendo, etc." I'm not saying that these things are bad, but all of the commercialism, radio, television, all of the things paraded before us are too much; we are inundated. You walk out into the streets of our cities, and there are billboards. Everybody is trying to get you to buy something from him or her. Everybody is trying to distract you and say, "No, it's

Gregory F. Bearstop

over here. You will be happy over here. You will be happy with this cologne, this makeup, wearing this type of style." It is too much. It's distracting you from asking this question: What is the greatest thing? So many people never find the happiness that they could have in life because they never ask the question. You can't answer a question that you never ask.

But there's good news. Whether we are conscious of it or not, we are all searching. We are searching for meaning, for something that gives us the best feeling, the greatest experience. As you search, learn about different things, and try some of them, you are uncovering a blueprint that will eventually lead to your happiness. You begin to find out what satisfies you and what doesn't. Then you may try to figure out a way to make the pleasure last longer. But as we go through life, we hopefully get tired of having the quick fix, a moment of pleasure, because this never gives us long-term fulfillment. This is slavery. When we get sick and tired of our captivity to temporary pleasure, then we begin to realize that the things of this world that do not last will never make us happy. How do you know if you have realized this? You know when you stop going after temporary things and you discover the treasure in the things that last. This treasure is your happiness.

Remember how elated you were as a kid when you got your first bicycle? You could go five or ten miles across town and back. Remember how good it felt to have that kind of freedom? Eventually when you became old enough to drive, you reached a teenager's heaven. You got a sense of fulfillment that seemed to last forever, because now you could go thousands of miles at speeds of 65 miles per hour and above. In life, most people are stuck in the bicycle phase of life in which they can get a quick fix or short-lived

Happiness That Is Guaranteed

pleasure. They do not realize that there are things in this life that can give them lasting fulfillment, thousands of miles of satisfaction forever.

Now you might say, "Wait a minute, there have been times when temporary satisfaction has fulfilled me. I have had some awesome experiences where sex made me happy." Do you think sex made you happy? It didn't. Sex gave you a thrill. But it didn't make you happy. Happiness is not isolated, sporadic experiences that make us feel good. You can feel great one minute and despondent the next, but I wouldn't call this happiness. Instead, happiness is a state of being that is an overall sense or feeling of completeness, fulfillment, and peace that comes from knowing that everything is all right. Although you may be going through difficult times, everything will be all right. Because you take on this attitude, indeed everything *is* all right, even in the midst of troubled times. You may know individuals deep in poverty who laugh and enjoy their lives, despite their condition. They are free because they do not let their unpleasant situations keep them from enjoying life. Whether they know it or not, they have reached within themselves and made connection with the things that last. That's what happiness is, making connection with things that last.

This is not a gimmick. It is not another "how to be successful and happy" book. This is the real thing. It does not involve money, expensive property, or the acquisition of numerous degrees. You do not have to be popular or even know someone who has fortune and fame. The only requirement for happiness is that you open your heart and mind. Right now you can be happier than you've ever been if you stop looking to things that don't last to make you happy and start to discover on your own the things that do.

Gregory F. Bearstop

Before we begin to deal specifically with things that last and how to connect with them, we first need to look at things that we are encouraged to pursue that will never give us happiness. There are four reasons why they will never fulfill us:

1. They do not last.
2. They become commonplace.
3. The satisfaction they do give is short-lived.
4. They keep us wanting more; therefore, we are never satisfied.

I encourage you to add to this list your own reasons why you think that the things that we are programmed to pursue will never make you happy. You can also use these four points as a set of criteria to help you to decide whether a particular thing is going to make you happy. Ask yourself: (1) Does it last? (2) Will it become commonplace, or will I take it for granted? (3) Will the satisfaction go away? (4) Will it leave me wanting more and therefore frustrate me?

Using these four points, let us see how society's trappings will never fulfill you. It is time to see these things as they are. In seeing, you can release your hold on them, and they will release their hold on you.

Therefore, the aim of this chapter is to encourage us to look at our lives and see the things that we are pursuing that are never really going to give us lives of happiness. In seeing, change begins to happen.

Happiness That Is Guaranteed

POSSESSIONS

Who wouldn't want to own elegant suits or dresses, fine jewelry, or the house or car of your dreams? And when you get them, in the beginning you're happy. But over time, the luster wears off. Your possessions don't command as much of your attention as they used to. They don't thrill you anymore.

Remember the first time you owned a car? Remember how elated you were, especially if it was new? You proudly displayed it before your friends. You were protective of it. If you're like me, you could be two blocks away from your car, and you would still be watching it. You were proud of owning it. However, two or three months later in the mall parking lot, someone has opened his or her car door into the side of yours. Now the first scratches appear. You are dismayed, frustrated, and even angry. As months go by and the car begins to show more signs of use, your initial elation subsides. You start to get used to your blemished car to the point where you begin to take it for granted. You don't wash it as much. You are making more trips to the repair shop. To top it off, you even let your friends eat in it. At this point, it has become part of the tapestry of your commonplace belongings. Eventually this process starts all over again when we look for another car. Ironically, we seem to go through this process with all the things we possess. Our material possessions, as much as we pursue them, never give us lasting happiness. They are susceptible to breakage, theft, fire, and time. They will become worn and will gradually change. Besides, we cannot take them with us when we die. Some people may be thinking that I am carrying this discussion too far, because they don't want lasting fulfillment from material possessions anyway. In fact, they only want temporary pleasure from things. This is fine. But the truth is this: If we only want temporary pleasure from material things, why do we pursue them like an obsession? I've *got* to have that dress, those shoes, or that car. I've got to have it, or I won't feel as important as those people who do have it. I am acting obsessively when I *have* to have something or I won't be happy. One explanation for this behavior may be that some people are trying to fulfill a desire for happiness through a cycle in which they constantly experience the joy and pleasure of buying something new. If they can keep this cycle in motion, they will constantly experience pleasure similar to the feeling of being happy, as long as they have the means or the money to obtain new possessions. However, the money will run out eventually, which will put them back where they started, unhappy and unfulfilled.

MONEY

Your search for happiness continues as you start to realize that possessions are not the answer. But most of us are still not convinced that things that do not last will never make us happy. So we begin to think that the problem isn't possessions, it's is a lack of money. Many of us are fooled by money. We think that if we have enough of it, we would be happy. Society reinforces this by constantly showing us pictures of wealthy people who seem fulfilled. They wear gold on their hands and around their necks. They are clean-cut and surrounded by luxury. Did you ever look at their faces? They are relaxed. Because of their wealth, they don't seem to have any worries. On their faces they carry the expression that everything is all right in their lives, which is exactly the definition of happiness. Remember, happiness

Happiness That Is Guaranteed

is a state of being that is an overall sense or feeling of completeness, fulfillment, and peace that comes from knowing that everything will be all right. Now, see how we're tricked: Suddenly money is linked with an overall or lasting sense of peace and a feeling of wholeness; but money can't buy lasting peace and wholeness. This is something that is already within us. The problem is that we don't know how to plug into it. We'll see how to do this in the chapters to come. However, one of the saddest things about how money fools us is that too many young people are trying to fit into the picture of wealth, which is a lie about how to get fulfillment. They are wearing the gold chains around their necks, driving the Lexuses, and trying to look sporty just like the wealthy. But there is another side. When the cameras are turned off and the makeup is removed, whether we are rich or poor, we all have to deal with life. Money cannot exempt us from dealing with the joys, losses, and frustrations in life; in fact, it can cause a lot of them. On one hand, if we rely on money for fulfillment and we have a lot of it, we can always come up with a reason for needing more. It's funny how our imaginations just come to life. Things that we never thought we needed suddenly become dire needs; therefore, the more money we have, the more we think of things to spend it on. Then we have to protect our money, so we need more money to protect our money. Then we need more money to protect the things we bought with our money. The more money we have, the more we need; therefore acquiring money can be frustrating because it seems that we can never get enough of it. On the other hand, it's frustrating if we have very little, because it seems that most of it goes toward paying bills. Therefore, on either end, we are never satisfied.

Gregory F. Bearstop

Large sums of money can contribute to your prosperity, but money cannot give you a sense of lasting fulfillment that edifies the core of your being. Money cannot love you or give you enduring peace; yet, advertisements and television commercials link excessive money with love, peace, and other priceless virtues. No amount of money can buy true love or peace, because if it could, you wouldn't know if it were genuine. Instead, money would become just another condition in order for you to love. Inherently, money is not bad; however, when it is misused to deceive people along the path to happiness, especially to become a vicarious God, it is very dangerous.

SEX

Since money isn't the answer, you may try to find fulfillment or compensate your desire for happiness through sex. Although it can be a tremendously pleasurable experience, it does not go on forever. It can tire you out; it is a pleasingly exhausting experience.

It too can become commonplace. If you watch the same sex scene in a movie every day for a month, you will become bored. Who would have heard of becoming bored with sex? However, if you are having sex often with the same partner over a long period, it will become dull and predictable, especially if that's all there is. On the other hand, if you are beginning to experiment with sex, you may have a seemingly insatiable appetite for it. In this case, you never get enough of it; you are never filled. A good example of this is a person who is preoccupied with pornography. She is always searching for the right centerfold or movie that will turn her on the most, but she never finds it, because she is constantly thinking that there has to be a centerfold or movie better than those she has already seen. As a result, she is never satisfied, because her happiness depends upon a cycle that is always going to leave her frustrated. We can also do this with people: When sex is disappointing, we begin to look for other partners. Even with a new partner, we may think in the back of our mind that there is probably someone else who could give us even more pleasure. But if we think this way with everyone we meet, we will never be content.

It is interesting how you can go to bed with a person you hardly know in order to relieve your sexual desires. You try to be so intensely physical with your partner. You kiss and you try to do everything possible to get into the other. Yet sex is about getting into the *heart* of each other. This is why after having sex with someone you hardly know, you may be physically satisfied, but you still feel empty inside. How can you get into the heart of someone you hardly know? For all you know, this person would throw you and your mother down a flight of stairs for a handful of money. Would you want to go to bed with someone like that? Yet when you are in the heart of another and he or she is in yours, sex has a quality about it that seems to last forever. This is the beginning of a committed relationship. A real sign of a committed relationship is that someone wants to be with *you*, instead of twelve people *like* you.

DRUGS

As a substance abuse counselor, I have heard various reasons why people use drugs, but the one reason that stands out is that these substances make you feel good, euphoric, happy. Now it is easy to look down on the drug addict and the alcoholic, but if you smoke or drink occasionally, you are just like them in the sense that you are trying to feel good too. Do you smoke or have a few beers because it causes pain? Certainly not. The point is that you put substances into your body that you don't need because they artificially do for you what you don't do for yourself naturally. It doesn't matter whether you smoke cigarettes, drink beer, or use narcotics; they are all drugs. A drug is any substance that changes your mood. It is easier to have a drink, pop a pill, or smoke a joint to feel good than it is to change one's mental state naturally (so we think). We want to feel good *immediately*. Fast, fast, fast! The problem is that the high doesn't last. It is important to know that you are always aiming to feel the high that you had when you first tried the drug, but you never get it. That's a frustrating adventure. However, the high that you *do* get, that rush of pleasure, becomes irresistible. It is as if you have stumbled upon the key to a perfect world within yourself. You visit there often, but not without paying an enormous price for the privilege. Over time, you need to increase the drug usage to sustain the high. But when you come down, you go through withdrawal symptoms such as fatigue, listlessness, severe headaches, vomiting, depression, and a host of other symptoms. If you were depressed before using, when you come down from the high, you will experience two and three times the depression you felt before.

Eventually, your freedom is taken away. You no longer control your drug habit. You no longer choose when and how much to use. You are on *its* schedule. You are at the mercy of the drug. When you are sick and hung over, it is hard to keep a job. When your drinking or drug use makes you violent, physically and verbally abusive, it is impossible to create and maintain a loving, nurturing environment for your family.

Drug abuse and dependence will cause self-defeating consequences. It is hard to feel happy when your drug use causes you to lose your job, home, friends, family, children, and self-respect. You can even lose your life, because continual use will cause deadly diseases such as cancer, heart disease, cirrhosis, dementia, and a host of other illnesses. If you are dealing drugs, you can lose your life even faster by wasting away in jail or by nameless bullets. The saddest part is that all you ever wanted was to be happy, but like many of us, you fell prey to things that do not last.

FAME AND SOCIETY'S VERSION OF SUCCESS

You have heard of many celebrities and popular figures who have achieved fame and fortune, but over time, they have either lost their wealth, had their reputations destroyed, or experienced both. Look at how O.J. Simpson has gone from having a reputation as one of America's most renowned athletes to a man struggling to hold on to his dignity. The lives of these celebrities demonstrate that our mundane achievements and assets do not guarantee happiness.

What society hails as success is fame and fortune. Turning to these trappings will never give you fulfillment. Please do not misunderstand this message. Money, expensive homes, merchandise, elegant clothes, fame, prestige, and other assets associated with success are good goals and worth pursuing, but they can't give you the signs of true success: happiness, peace, joy, and all the wonderful virtues of trust, hope, and true love. They can never give me internal success, which is the feeling that I do not desire anything to validate me; I do not have to prove to myself that I am worthwhile, a priceless gift to the world. Instead, I believe and feel the truth, which is that the world would be less beautiful and lacking in greatness if you or I were not in it; nothing of the world, things that end, can give us this feeling. A test of happiness is whether I can go without society's luxurious trappings of success and feel at peace, complete, or not need anything worldly to feel worthwhile.

SIGNIFICANT RELATIONSHIPS

As you journey through life, you will discover that material possessions, money, success, and other finite things can only satisfy you for a short while, but they cannot fill the void within you. They cannot take away the loneliness, boredom, or whatever lack you feel inside. In an attempt to fill the void, you may turn to relationships. In your experiences, you notice that when you are with a close friend or someone you like, often the loneliness goes away and the void seems filled. This is when you start to believe that when you find the man or woman of your dreams, then you will be happy. No, you won't! Even if you find the man or woman of your dreams, you won't be happy. Sure, you will have many precious moments when you will be wrapped up in the love and caring that you will feel for each other, but there will also be times when you will get angry, when you cannot stand being in the same room with each other. You certainly won't be happy during times like these. So now you are back to having sporadic moments of feeling fulfilled in your relationship. This is not happiness. Remember that happiness is a state of being, a state of mind that no matter what happens, everything is going to be all right, and indeed is all right. This is a feeling that you can always have, whether you are in a significant relationship or not. If you have this state of mind and you are in a relationship, you are probably happy or moving in the right direction. However, the point is that no man or woman can cause you to have or not have a peaceful state of being. Only *you* decide that.

Relationships, fulfilling as they are, cannot guarantee our happiness. Even when you fall in love, so many things can go wrong. No one can absolutely guarantee that your involvement with significant others will last. You must always keep this reality in front of you. Therefore, it is best to enjoy the people in your life and to work toward lasting relationships, but do not ultimately depend on them for lasting happiness. Enjoy them, appreciate what you have, but do not count on them for ultimate fulfillment that lasts forever.

I think that people are devastated when relationships do not work out, mainly because they have not found sources in their lives that can guarantee lasting happiness.

I remember that several years ago, I had a friend who was married to a very handsome man. During their marriage, her husband ran off with another woman. My friend was heartbroken and devastated. She never seemed to come to terms with the whole ordeal. She became so deep in despondency that eventually she committed suicide. I cannot help wondering whether she might be alive today if she had not depended so heavily upon her husband to fulfill her. Tragic stories like this one remind us that even our relationships cannot promise lasting fulfillment.

At this point, we have looked at how the things we are inclined to pursue can never give us lasting happiness. We have seen that the reasons why they cannot fulfill us are *(1)*

Gregory F. Bearstop

They do not last. (2) They become commonplace. (3) The satisfaction that they do give is short-lived. (4) They keep us wanting more; therefore, we are never satisfied.

Finally, there is a fifth reason that is extremely important to pay close attention to. This reason is that *too much emphasis on the things of the world can eventually kill us*. Let's take a closer look at this.

When we consider our lives and where our energy, time, and attention are expended, we notice that a lot of it is used to serve things that will never give us lasting joy. For instance, we spend much of our time trying to take care of things that have finality. We buy clothes, but they have to be washed, tailored, and taken to the cleaners. Our possessions at home need to be dusted, vacuumed, cleaned, mopped, repaired, replaced, and so on. If you own a car, just look at the maintenance schedule of your car manual to see the care it requires. In addition, sometimes we have to work two or three jobs to earn the income to take care of our possessions. The labor and the enormous energy that this process consumes causes many of us to live very stressful lives. Because of the unnecessary exertion that we put into things and situations that are not going to give us lasting joy, we become stressed to the point where it is making us sick. It has been proven time and time again that stress causes serious diseases that are fatal. Too many people are dying unnecessarily because they are wearing themselves out in pursuit of things and situations that will never fulfill them.

Fortunately, there are times when we give ourselves a break from the stress; however, sometimes we don't give ourselves the break we need and really desire. We try to eliminate our stress by returning to those same pleasures that didn't last because we really don't know where else to turn. So we come full circle: To get some relief, we go back to buying toys, killing ourselves to make more money, or trying to get rewards from society. We look for more sex or find a new drug on the market. Just as before, they may give us pleasure for a short while, but then stress returns. Tired of this unending cycle, the core of our being cries out: "If my possessions, money, success, drugs, sex, significant relationships, and other short-lived pleasures cannot give me lasting happiness, then what can? What can?" All we hear in response is silence. Nothing. We interpret the nothing, the emptiness, to mean that temporary things are all there is, so we might as well make the best of them. Therefore, we return to the unending cycle of relying on these things for fulfillment. But there is a reason we cannot hear beyond the silence: We adhere to three major beliefs or philosophies of life that keep us stuck in the unending cycle. These beliefs reinforce each other, which makes it almost impossible to break free from our reliance on immediate pleasures.

THREE UNFULFILLING PHILOSOPHIES

The first belief or philosophy that keeps us in the unending cycle is the belief that *if you are going to die anyway, you might as well try to get as much pleasure out of this life as possible*. This reinforces a need for immediate gratification. Because we are only seeing the immediate, we place little to no emphasis on things that last. We are not interested in them. We want things that are going to give us immediate gratification because life is going to end; life is moving fast. I want to enjoy myself as much as possible. I am not thinking about any consequences beyond this life. As far as I'm concerned, it all could be an illusion.

Gregory F. Bearstop

This philosophy is stemming from the belief that when I die, that is the end. There is an uncertainty about what is on the other side of death, (if there *is* another side). So we remain stuck. Our goal is to get as much pleasure as we possibly can, despite the consequences. The consequences really do not matter. The ultimate consequence is death, no matter how you slice it. We can see evidence of this as we deal with the AIDS crisis. There are marches, television commercials, fund-raisers, and many different activities going on to heighten the awareness of the consequences of HIV and AIDS. However, many people are still infecting one another at alarming rates, even after all of this information has been publicized. What philosophy is behind this? Again, immediate gratification. I want to go to bed with this person, and that is all that matters. I am wasting my time thinking about consequences, because I am going to die anyway, whether it is by AIDS, cancer, old age, a tumor, smoking, or something else.

The second philosophy that assists in locking us into this cycle of going after temporary things is the belief that *there isn't enough to go around; there isn't an abundance.* There is a lack in the world and in me. Yet everyone wants things immediately. Fast, fast, fast! Because I believe that there isn't enough, I better get mine first, because if you get there before I do, I lose out. An example is our workforce. Presidents of some companies are making $25 million a year. I am not saying that there is something necessarily wrong with this, but there is something wrong when the people who have worked to make you that $25 million have to live on $20,000 annually. Families are literally surviving on $20,000, as compared with $25 million. You see, I've got to get mine, because somehow there is not enough money to go around. There are not enough resources that could be shared. This dynamic keeps people struggling, keeps the cycle active, because we feel that there is not enough.

Another way of emphasizing my point is by showing you a person who approaches others out of a sense of abundance. When I was 13 years old, I worked a summer job cleaning trash out of alleys in Washington, D.C. One day, a girl noticed me struggling to clean an alley in 100-degree weather. She called out to me to come into her home to get a glass of ice-cold water. As I entered the kitchen, I was struck by the poverty in which she lived. There were only three wooden chairs and a badly worn table. Her grandmother sat in front of an open refrigerator to keep cool. Yet despite their meager surroundings, her two younger sisters and older brother seemed to be in a cheerful mood. She handed me a glass of ice-cold water that seemed to come out of nowhere. I was moved to tears as I thought how this beautiful girl could offer me water when she had nothing. Certainly, her grandmother could have benefited from the water she gave me. Yet, in her home, there was a sense that there was enough to go around, enough even to reach out to a thirsty stranger.

The third philosophy that keeps us from fulfillment is the belief that *if I cannot see it, it does not exist*. Don't talk to me about something that I cannot see. Subsequently, that is exactly what we do. We go after things that we can physically see, which makes sense to us. Give me something with substance. Substance for us is something that I can see and experience with my five senses. If it goes beyond this, I am not interested; you are wasting my time. In substance abuse counseling, I would often refer to the twelve steps of Alcoholics Anonymous, which are based on spirituality and the incorporation of a Higher Power into one's life. And when I begin to introduce this concept of Higher Power and how we need to plug into something beyond ourselves to help release us from our addiction, inevitably someone lets out a big yawn. "Don't talk to me about God or a Higher Power; I can't see any of that stuff. This is like grabbing the wind; it's not concrete." When you mention Higher Power or God, people yawn unless they get into trouble, someone dies, they're in dire straights, or they're suffering tremendously; then they call on God. But when we find out who is sleeping with whom, oh everyone is interested now. Who did what to whom? No one is yawning. We want the juicy stuff. We want something that we can physically grab onto, something we can see. We are skeptical about going after things we cannot see, because for all we know, it could be an illusion. It could be a waste of our time. There is no real evidence. We'd rather deal with things we are used to, even if they don't fulfill us. This is real for us. So we continue in a cycle that goes nowhere.

There are other beliefs that perpetuate this cycle, and I encourage you to add your own. However, the three philosophies we have just discussed are some of the main beliefs that hinder our fulfillment.

Is there any hope of getting out of this cycle? I understand that I am trapped in it. I see how it happens. I see the beliefs that keep me stuck here. But how do I get out of it? I really do want to be happy. I want to get out of this cycle of trying to get lasting fulfillment from temporary pleasure. But how? The truth is that if we are going to get out of it, we are going to need something strong enough to influence our thinking, to jolt us to change our actions. We need something strong enough to eject us out of the revolving door. It is as though we are in a fixed

Happiness That Is Guaranteed

orbit from which we cannot deviate, because if we did, it would upset what we have gotten used to. When we change for the better, it does require some growing pains, some adjustment. Any type of change isn't comfortable. It takes getting used to. Usually when our lives change for the better, it doesn't necessarily happen by someone talking to us. It doesn't happen by someone yelling at us or telling us to get our life together. No, that is reinforcement for the same old behavior. We don't like to be told what to do. What usually gets our attention and catapults us out of the cycle is crisis; that's the reality. I am not talking about any crisis. I am talking about a situation that really jolts you. I am referring to a crisis that really gets you to face the question raised in the beginning of this chapter: What is the meaning of your life? For everyone, the crisis is different. Some people need to have a near-death experience. For others, it may take a crisis of an illness or a depression. For still others, it maybe that they wake up one morning and they are sick and tired of the way their life is going. And that is enough to launch them on a course to a new, exciting, rejuvenating way of life. It is a crossroads that all of us need to face. If you are tired of being unhappy, you have arrived at the crossroads. The fact that you have picked up this book and you want to know how to bring more joy into your life is a crossroads. And it is a good place to be. When you have suffered enough, change begins to happen, because you can't take it anymore; you have had enough. You are tired of depending upon others to be in a good mood in order for you to feel good. It is certainly hard to feel happy when someone is yelling at you in a heated rage. Instead, you want what that girl had that allowed her to give a stranger a drink of water when she had little to nothing. You are tired of only getting momentary satisfaction from possessions, money, sex, fame, drugs, and significant others, when deep down within yourself, you really want lasting fulfillment. You may have put up with this for months or even years, but there comes a day when you cannot take it anymore. And I say to you, don't take it anymore.

CHAPTER 2
CRISIS

Six years ago after making some exciting plans for self development, I was suddenly faced with one of the most draining situations in my life. My family and I received news that my mother, at age 58, had developed a tumor inside her spinal cord at the base of her neck. The doctors could not determine whether it was malignant or benign. It was impossible to get a sample of the tumor without causing further nerve damage and paralysis. In two months, my mother lost the use of her legs, arms, and hands. Consequently, most of the responsibility to care for her was left to me. My two brothers helped, but deep down I believe that our mother's illness was too painful for them to deal with on a consistent basis. I too felt this way at times, but if I did not take on the full responsibility of caring for her, who would?

Every day I felt like I was working two or three jobs. I would return home from my full-time job to care for our mother. I was glad to do what I could; however, over time, the daily chores began to overwhelm me. These chores involved cooking, cleaning, and providing constant medical attention. All of her meals were fed to her. She needed to be catheterized every six hours. Transferring her from her wheelchair to her bed and vice versa was an incredible task. She woke up several times at night either because she was uncomfortable or because she was suffering from fevers.

A few months later, the doctors decided to give her radiation therapy in an attempt to shrink the tumor. Fortunately, the radiation restored my mother's use of her

Gregory F. Bearstop

arms and hands, but that was all. Several months later, she once again lost the use of her right arm. Because the doctors had exhausted the amount of radiation treatment that they could give her, I feared that she would also lose the use of her left arm. This would have forewarned of an imminent death. I had to do something. There is no way that you can watch your mother deteriorate and not be torn apart by the sight. In order to hang on and not fall to pieces, I began to search for something that might make the situation better. I started reading and talking to people about how I could prevent my mother's paralysis from worsening. Finally, a friend encouraged me to start juicing, which is an excellent way of extracting juice from fruits and vegetables. One hundred percent of the vitamins and minerals that the body needs for optimal functioning and healing is in the juice of fruits and vegetables. Consequently, I began to read Jay Kordich's book, *The Juiceman's Power of Juicing*, where I learned that carrot-cantaloupe juice has one of the highest concentrations of beta carotene, which helps eliminate toxins in our cells and protect us from a variety of cancers. I also learned that juice made from green leafy plants such as spinach and broccoli contains chlorophyll, which helps to reduce tumor growth. Immediately, I ran out and bought a juice machine. I started my mother on a diet of carrot-cantaloupe juice and carrot-broccoli juice. Two years later, my mother still has use of her left arm, and her condition has not worsened.

My mother is now stabilized in a nursing home, although we do not know for how long. My family and I visit her every day. It is still difficult seeing her in a nursing home; however, I can deal with it a little better now because I feel that through the grace of God, her life has been extended. So I continue to juice. On the weekends, I take her to the mall, and if we are feeling adventurous, we might spend the weekend in Ocean City, Maryland. The best thing about all of this is that it keeps her in good spirits.

I share this experience because it was one of the major stepping stones that put me on the path to fulfillment and happiness. As I was going through the stress and turmoil associated with my mother's illness, I did not see any light at the end of the tunnel. Often I felt so overwhelmed by responsibilities and discontent that I was afraid I would end up in the hospital. But it was the pain of watching my mother deteriorate that prompted me to act. I began to search for a way to make the situation better. That is the purpose of crisis, to get us to search. This is how my mother's illness has put me on the path to fulfillment. It prompted me not only to search for something to make her condition better but also to search for a better way of dealing with suffering, pain, hurt, and depression. Through this crisis and the subsequent challenges, I learned how to experience anger, suffering, and depression and, at the same time, feel peace and fulfillment. We will talk about how to do this in the chapters to follow. For now, it is important to realize that the path to peace and fulfillment begins with crisis. The one jewel contained in crisis is that it prompts us to search and to ask questions that get us to come out of ourselves and expand our vision. As we do this, we learn how to obtain peace and fulfillment, not only when things are going well but also when times are hard.

All of us at one time or another are confronted with crisis. In fact, right now you may be in the middle of one. You may have just lost a loved one. You may be enduring a bad relationship. Some of you are hurting because friends, whom you once trusted, betrayed you. Others are lonely because they cannot find suitable companionship. If you are going through a crisis, you may feel like you are being torn apart. You may feel like you are in the dark. Because there doesn't seem to be any place you can turn to help you resolve the problem, the situation may get worse. It's painful; however, the pain becomes the crucial factor in a crisis.

When a difficult situation hurts enough, you begin to search for something that might make it better. You feel a little better in a crisis when you are at least searching for a solution, rather than doing nothing. That is the purpose of crisis, to get you to search. It wakes you up out of your sleep and gets you to go beyond yourself to find out what else is out there. It gets you to see things that you couldn't see before, to learn things that you didn't know before. It lights a fire under you and gets you to come out of your comfortable surroundings in order to find real fulfillment. This is the way that crisis is always nudging you toward fulfillment. Sometimes in response to crisis, we do not act effectively. We revert to the cycle that we talked about in chapter I, in which we try to find relief by constantly going after things that offer temporary fulfillment. For instance, when a loved one dies, some people cope by using drugs, or they get drunk and shut down. But when they sober up, the problem is still there. The person is still dead, and they still have to deal with the pain of this reality. When we are stuck in the cycle of relying on sex, money, popularity, and short-lived pleasures, we can't help ourselves or anyone else as much as we could if we opted to learn how to obtain peace from our crises in spite of our pain. What could we have shared with anyone about how to get real fulfillment? Nothing. Someone who has a sense of peace and security every day, no matter what happens, is going to be able to help himself or herself and others more than someone who only lives for moment-to-moment satisfaction. We are free to remain stuck in the cycle, but, at some point, we must realize that even if we go backwards, this is not solving the problem. It's keeping us stuck. Nothing changes. We rob ourselves of joy that can illumine our lives. Therefore, when we are in pain and we are looking for relief, we ought not search haphazardly; instead, our search needs to be focused on looking for things that have substance and longevity. Being focused in this way helps us to see more possibilities for making a difficult situation better. It helps us to look at the wider picture. For instance, I could have chosen to deal with my mother's illness by simply visiting her daily in the nursing home. She certainly would have appreciated my presence. But because I was also focused on how I could provide long-term impact on her condition, I was prompted to go beyond just visiting her. Through reading and talking with others, I found out what was available to arrest her paralysis. This is how I stumbled upon juicing, which has helped sustain my mother's life to this day, six years after being diagnosed with a tumor. The juicing was a little step that showed me what can happen when I search, not haphazardly but specifically, looking for things that endure and give long-term results. Without this kind of searching, most likely my mother would be dead.

The main point is that when you are in a crisis and you begin to search for relief, begin to look for things that endure and give long-term results. When you do this, you will be able to see the wider picture, which will give you more options to deal with the problem effectively. The things that we thought were impossible become possible, and now our minds have been broadened to receive them.

Gregory F. Bearstop

Whereas before, crisis was a big annoyance; we couldn't see any meaning in it.

A few years, ago I worked for an employer who wasn't very pleasant to me and my coworkers. He snapped at us and often talked down to us. As time went on, the company began to fail. My employer didn't try to revive it; he had given up. Because he no longer seemed to care much about the stress of running the business, he didn't try to control us anymore, and strangely he became more polite. He became more carefree and relaxed. People actually started to like him. Because we felt freer to do our work, morale improved, and we became more productive. As a result, the company began to flourish and yield record profits. Our employer recognized how his kindness contributed to our stress-reduced environment and our overall success. Since his realization, he has treated us respectfully, and the company continues to thrive.

My employer may not have changed his ways intentionally. But when he saw the business failing, it was disheartening and painful enough to cause him to let go of his malice and treat his staff with kindness and respect. Witnessing the results of his changed behavior, he started to think of the long-term effects of being supportive of the staff. This was the lesson he learned from the crisis of needing to rejuvenate his failing business. Because he started to look at the long-term results of supporting his staff, the crisis began to improve dramatically. This lesson has also benefited his relationship with his fiancée. They listen to each other more. He doesn't try to control her; instead, they can talk through their differences, rather than trying to impose their opinions upon each other.

When you find ways of making a difficult situation better for the long term, crisis is not as threatening as it used to be. You may find a way of resolving a crisis by changing the way that you think about the situation, concentrating more on the positive aspects, or by being patient and kind to the people involved. However, the main point is that as you resolve the situation, not only are you becoming a better person but you are also developing skills that will enable you to deal effectively with crisis in the future. Just like in the example of my employer, if his business had not failed, he may not have become a better person who could foster healthier relationships. This is why crises are like a video game. You have to overcome one level before you move to the next. And if you do not master a particular level, you have to constantly repeat it until you learn the lessons that will allow you to move beyond it. Struggling with my mother's illness gave me the opportunity to learn those lessons. Because if I didn't, I would be a person who is alive on the outside, but very dead on the inside. This is why crisis is not a dead end, but a means to an end. In this way, it can teach us three major lessons that are essential for becoming a better person and putting us on the path to fulfillment:

1. Recognize that crises are stepping stones leading to happiness.
2. Be willing to pursue happiness through your trials with all your heart.
3. Be willing to go within yourself and cultivate the skills and qualities that have enabled you to overcome crises in the past.

Gregory F. Bearstop

1. Recognize that crises are stepping stones leading to happiness.

It is difficult to understand how crises can be stepping stones leading to happiness. When you are going through a crisis, it is very painful. Even when you have gone through trials and overcome them, you may not always be satisfied with the results. Sometimes the outcome of an onerous situation leaves you feeling angry, frustrated, and unfairly treated. For instance, if, during the course of an arduous relationship, your significant other decides to pursue another relationship, you may feel distraught and heartbroken. Where is the happiness in this? Therefore, we need to understand three things about crisis. First, crises are *stepping stones* to happiness; they do not yield happiness as an immediate result. Second, the outcome of crisis does not always determine whether you will be fulfilled. Third, what matters most in a crisis is not the outcome, but what you learned that can further your self-development and fulfillment. You may have learned which objects to avoid or a better strategy to use in a similar situation; however, if you learn nothing and refuse to see anything in your trials, then your struggles are in vain, useless.

Some people think that our lives would be better without crises. I wonder. For without some challenges, we would not grow and mature. We would learn very few of the real lessons in life. Even the lack of challenges would become a crisis because we would be bored, too comfortable and too lazy to pursue the things that matter most in life.

Life is not about just existing; it is about being happy. Life gives you crises and challenges to wake you up from becoming comfortable with the same old things and to

Happiness That Is Guaranteed

learn to pursue the things that matter most: your fulfillment and happiness. Therefore, everyone is called to be happy. This is not forced on you; you have the freedom to refuse it. But, if you respond to the call, you will find the road that leads to lasting happiness.

2. Be willing to pursue happiness through your trials with all your heart.

Often we may feel discouraged, especially when the outcome of a difficult situation is not what we desired. We are frustrated and tremendously disappointed. Sometimes we feel like we have failed, and we begin to communicate to ourselves the message that there is very little that we can accomplish. At this point, it becomes very easy to give up our pursuit of happiness and to live a life complaining about why we are unhappy.

As we work through our problems, we may gain insight about how to avoid similar situations, but we may not feel that what we are learning is directing us toward our fulfillment. When we feel this way, first we need to exercise a little patience. Do not try to force happiness. Allow yourself to go through a process, possibly similar to the one described in this book. Talk to a friend about your problem, because he or she may be able to recognize avenues to fulfillment when your vision is cloudy. Ask yourself, what can I learn from this crisis that can make my life better and fulfilling? Remember that there is always something to be learned in every crisis that can make your life happier.

Second, when you do not get the results that you are looking for, remember that there is no such thing as failure, unless you stop trying. These setbacks are opportunities that will bring you closer to happiness. No one I've ever known has found happiness without first experiencing setbacks; therefore, never give up. Everyone who tries to find happiness and never gives up will indeed find it. Remember that if you keep rolling the dice, you will eventually come up with sevens. Colonel Sanders' Kentucky Fried Chicken business would not exist if he did not receive 1,004 rejections of his recipe before receiving that one "yes" on the 1,005th try. If you want something, claim it and do not look back.

3. Be willing to cultivate the skills and qualities that have enabled you to overcome crises in the past.

Let's try a little exercise. Take a moment and think of a crisis that you have overcome. What was the crisis about? Who were the people involved? What were your strengths, skills, and qualities that helped you to deal with the situation effectively? One way to recognize your skills that you may otherwise overlook is to ask yourself: What were my positive thoughts that helped me to get through the crisis? What insights did I arrive at? If the answer to these questions helped you to get through your crisis, then those answers are your strengths, skills, and qualities. Take a moment to list these strengths and feel free to add other skills and qualities that come to mind.

1.
2.
3.
4.
5.

How can you use these strengths, skills, and qualities to help you overcome a difficult situation that you may be experiencing right now?

You may have dealt better with a crisis when you began to concentrate more on the positive thoughts, rather than on the negative thoughts that sapped your energy. For example, I used to have a horrendous time preparing speeches. I was always concentrating on negative thoughts about how I may not say the right thing or about how I wouldn't inspire anyone. Consequently, it would take me days just to write one page. However, after wrestling with this issue, I realized that I was struggling with my confidence. So I began to focus on the inspiring speeches that I had given. As a result, I began to relax more. I started to give myself positive thoughts and messages about how I would know the right phrases and words to use. If I wasn't sure what to say, I could always use techniques like brainstorming. I began to feel like there was always some technique that I could use to come up with the perfect words. When I wrote future speeches with these thoughts in mind, eventually the words began to flow naturally and eloquently.

Therefore, crisis can teach you the benefits of positive thinking. Positive thoughts are essential for overcoming crisis because they are a catalyst for putting you in a relaxed state of mind. When you are relaxed, you can think more clearly. You have the agility and flexibility in your thought patterns that can lead you to make many momentary sound decisions in challenging situations. Think back to a situation in your life when you were tense because you were filled with many negative thoughts. What kind of behavior did you display? Crisis is like running a race. If you run focused on negative thoughts such as what if I don't win or maybe I'm not good enough, then you lock up; you become tense. You won't be limber enough to muster speed and to stretch out with the large strides needed to win.

In order to concentrate on positive thoughts in difficult times, first acknowledge that the negative thoughts are not going to help you to move through the crisis; they are only going to cause you more pain. Second, remember a difficult challenge in the past that you overcame. Relish in the fact that you got through it. Recognize how strong and capable you are. Concentrate on the positive thoughts you had then. Relive the victory. Third, continue to allow your confidence to build until you feel both confident and relaxed. Fourth, now while you are in a confident-relaxed state, begin to brainstorm constructive ways of dealing with the difficult situation confronting you.

Another key point: Who are the people surrounding me? Whose influence helped me to get through a crisis? What was my environment like? Was it very stressful? What aspect of my environment helped me? Did I have a peaceful space to go to to help me quiet down so that I could think clearer? Was I always in chaos, in an environment where people were yelling at each other and I couldn't get away?

Do not take these things for granted, because they are pivotal to overcoming crisis now and in the future. If I don't pick out the strengths, the qualities that really helped me to get through past crises, then I may not cultivate and use some of those same skills and qualities now.

In summary, crisis helps you to break free of a cycle in which you have become comfortable with relying upon short-lived pleasures that can never give you lasting fulfillment. When you experience enough pain or discomfort in a crisis, then you begin to search for a way to make the situation better. However, if you are going to be effective, your search cannot be a haphazard one; instead, it must be focused on looking for an outcome that yields long-term positive results. This is the kind of searching that expands your vision and makes you a wiser and better person. It is in expanding your vision that you find the path to fulfillment.

CHAPTER 3

EXPANDING YOUR VISION OF HAPPINESS

To find happiness in our lives, it is essential that you and I expand our vision about what happiness is. We need to do this because our beliefs play a significant role in shaping our reality. For example, many of us believe that we won't be happy until we find the man or woman of our dreams. However, if this person does not come along until ten or fifteen years from now, or if you never find him or her, are you going to be unhappy for the rest of your life? Would you live the rest of your life with the same joy that you would have had if you were happily married? Therefore, the first step we need to take to expand our vision of happiness is to cultivate an understanding about what it is. We need to define happiness so that we broaden the possibilities of bringing more joy into our lives than we would if we held on to beliefs that limit our fulfillment. If you are holding on to a belief that is preventing you from bringing more joy into your life, you're never going to have it. Life is about expanding one's vision. If you are not growing and expanding every day, you are not living!

Challenging Our Beliefs About Happiness

Some of you believe that happiness is lasting joy that you may experience in another life after death because there are too many problems in this life. It seems that once things are going well, here comes some dilemma or crisis to disrupt your peaceful balance. Yet if you bring the belief that you cannot be happy in this life to every problem situation, then you will never find happiness. This belief

Happiness That Is Guaranteed

will shape and color each problem you face so that it actually impedes your ability to effectively handle the situation. As a result, a situation that could have brought peace into your life ends up causing prolonged discomfort.

I remember a woman who used crack while trying to raise a sixteen-year-old daughter, and two sons, ages five and two. Often her sixteen-year-old daughter was left for three days at a time to care for her brothers while her mother went on a crack binge; the children would suffer by not having three meals a day, clean clothes, and a sanitary environment. The mother told me that she used crack because she wanted to escape the hardships of being a single parent on welfare. She believes that she is not going to be happy in this life, and therefore she escapes to a world of crack addiction to feel some fulfillment. This is why so many people turn to alcohol, drugs, and other unhealthy activities. They do these things out of despair of ever finding happiness. This belief manifests itself in many forms.

You may be working on a job you don't like, yet you have been doing it for years. Why? Why have you been doing something you don't like day after day? Sure, the job provides a paycheck. But is it worth being unhappy for when you could make the same amount of money or more working a job you love? At the heart of it all, what keeps us in these jobs and situations is the belief that we are not going to be happy in this life; we are not going to feel an inner core of peace and joy, for whatever reason. Therefore, it really does not matter if we pour ourselves into jobs or situations we really don't care much about. Ultimately, one job is not much different from another. Everywhere we go, we find something wrong. Either the supervisor is too uptight, the coworkers are incompetent, or there is some other defect. These are all excuses to justify why we cannot experience happiness in our lives. When you are working at a job you love, the supervisor, coworkers, and challenges are not the central issue; your happiness is not contingent upon them. Because of your enthusiasm and joy for what you do, if problems and challenges do arise, you will have the stamina and know-how to arrive at a resolution. But in order to welcome opportunities into your life that will contribute to your happiness, you must cultivate the belief that you can be happy in this life.

Another belief that limits our happiness is believing that happiness comes from outside ourselves. We look to things outside of us and latch onto them in the hope that they will be a constant source of joy and fulfillment. But as we said in chapter 1, these things are not reliable. You cannot turn to them at every moment and expect them to offer some sense of joy and comfort. As we look for happiness outside ourselves, we avoid going within ourselves, which is where happiness lies. Inside all of us there is an inner voice or an inner consciousness that knows what will make you happy and it knows how to obtain it. But we don't often listen to that nagging voice. No one knows better than you what gets you excited and brings you tremendous joy.

Yet we are programmed, conditioned to think that things outside of us will fulfill us. We develop this pattern from the messages that we receive from the media, television, radio, and our closest friends. I was listening the other day to a radio station that played love songs. It struck me that most of these love songs were filled with a bunch of lies. The message that these songs are sending out is not consistent with reality. Whitney Houston sings, "You are all the man that I need." And Luther Vandross sings, "You are all the woman that I need." Callers would dedicate

Happiness That Is Guaranteed

songs to people whom they would describe as their whole world. Such statements are fallacies. No person can be your entire world, your everything. To expect our significant other to live up to such a sublime image is an extreme burden, and it results in disaster. Yet this is one of the main reasons why there are so many unhappy people. We expect one person to make us happy, to fulfill our needs. Deep down, we know that no man or woman can be our everything and make us happy. But unable to accept the fact that happiness originates in a person such as yourself, we hold on tenaciously to the possibility that there has to be someone out there who can make me happy. Eventually, we may meet someone who makes us feel like we are the greatest person in the world. We do whatever we can for them because it gives us another opportunity to be involved with someone we feel excited about. But in time, these things get old. We become accustomed to their predictable ways. We notice things about them that we don't find attractive. The spark felt in the beginning diminishes. Then we begin to think that if only we could do more for the relationship, we can rekindle the spark. Yet we end up wearing ourselves out trying to fulfill each other's needs, usually at the expense of neglecting our own. Our companion may become too exhausted to do the little sweet things that they used to do. Subsequently, we think that we have chosen the wrong companion. We say to ourselves, "This person is different from when I first met him or her." But the reality is that our companion isn't much different; for the most part, people do not change over night. We have not necessarily chosen the wrong companion. Just about all relationships run this course if we are looking for the other to make us happy. What we are coming face to face with is the opportunity to accept our significant other as a real person who has limitations, not as the person whom we hardly knew, which made it easier for him or her to match our image of the perfect companion. Once you face the real person, then you can decide whether you want to live with the good and bad qualities of this individual. In every relationship, you have to face the real person, who is not going to give you inner fulfillment, inner joy that depends on no one. Therefore, we are unhappy not because we cannot find the right person, but because we are going outside ourselves, looking for another person to deny the fact that he or she has limits so that he or she can fulfill us. Because we are limited, our capacity to make someone happy is also limited. Therefore, a relationship works when two people come together not to make each other happy, but to affirm and share the joy that they already possess within their hearts. Thus the only way that you are going to find happiness is to look within yourself.

Self-Love Is the Means to Happiness.

One of the most significant ways of going within yourself is through self-love; therefore, the second step to expanding your vision of happiness is exercising self-love. This concept sometimes seems so far removed from us; it's not tangible. It's abstract. We think of many things that we would like to do for ourselves, but sometimes the thought does not get translated into action. We accept as a given that we automatically care for ourselves. As a result, we abuse ourselves by neglecting our needs. We even act like a neglected person. How often do you think about whether you have cared properly for yourself in the course of a day? I know that most of us have some degree of care for ourselves. At the same time, we often exercise a considerable degree of self-abuse and neglect. We do this in two ways.

First, we do not become our own best friend. One way of being your own best friend so that self-love is more real and tangible is by employing a little bit of Gestalt therapy. What you would do is picture yourself as your best friend. If you are alone, it may help to place an empty chair in front of you and picture yourself sitting in that chair. Now ask yourself: How have I allowed others to drain me at the expense of casting my own needs aside as if they do not matter? How am I contributing to my own pain or dissatisfaction? Once you answer these questions, then ask yourself: Would I do to my best friend the things that I have allowed others to do to me? Would I do to my best friend the things that I have done to myself? How would I advise my best friend in order to resolve a difficult situation? Whatever you would do for your best friend, do it for yourself. If you are not your own best friend, how can you be anyone else's?

The second way in which we wear ourselves out is by constantly doing a lot for other people, to the point of having nothing to give to ourselves. Often we are really unaware of how much of our time and energy we give away. Out of 168 hours in a week, we give approximately 55 hours per week to our job, which includes preparing ourselves for work and the roundtrip commute. We sleep for an average of 49 hours per week, and we give an average of 40 hours per week to family members, friends, the maintenance of our home, our possessions, and our general life-style. This leaves us with about 24 hours per week to devote to ourselves. However, depending upon how many dependents you have, you may be fortunate to get 5 or 10 hours per week for yourself. We benefit indirectly from most of the things and people in whom we invest. Also, we may even enjoy the many ways through which we give of ourselves. However, in order to continue to do this, the question is: How are you giving directly to yourself?

Most of our time is spent absorbed in fulfilling everyone else's needs; however, we forget that the world runs on self-love and that a lack of it is the world's demise. When we talk about caring for yourself, we are not talking about being preoccupied with yourself to the point where you are only concerned with your needs. Instead, we are talking about caring for your needs in order to better serve the needs of others. This distinguishes self-love from selfishness. When you go within yourself, you begin to open the floodgate to happiness. The means to do this is self-love and appreciation. You cannot care about anything or anyone if you don't start at home with self.

The third step in expanding your vision of happiness is actually part of the second step, but because it is so crucial to your happiness, it has to receive special attention. The third step is to give time and energy back to yourself. This is a matter of life and death. Many people have literally died from the cumulative effects of not giving enough time and energy to themselves to do life-giving things that they enjoy.

In chapter 2, I related how my mother was deteriorating from a spinal cord tumor, but I remained quiet about some major factors that I believe contributed to her condition. So often we do not want to look at what we have done and what we are doing now that will cause grave consequences in the future. My mother is the type of person who is always on the go, working herself to death while giving little attention to her needs for rejuvenation. I began to follow in her footsteps.

As my mother was being stabilized in a nursing home, I was still wearing myself out trying to be attentive to her while working full-time and fulfilling other responsibilities. I had reached a point of becoming angry from extreme exhaustion. I suppose that this would be called a codependent relationship. But like Pavlov's dogs, when my mother sounded, I came running. I visited her practically every day. I had given up all my weekends. On Saturdays and Sundays, if I was not spending an average of six hours visiting her, I was taking her for a drive in the car. On some weekends, we would even go for an overnight stay in Ocean City, Maryland, or to some other renowned resort within a day's drive. These things were nice ways of caring for my mother. I had no problems being a good son. But I was not the best son that I could have been because I was caring for mom at the expense of doing harm to myself. I was exhausting myself and compromising my health, which left me unhappy and angry. I was especially angry at my family members because I felt that if they had spent some weekends with her, it would have given me a break. However, a close friend woke me up to reality when he firmly stated, "Greg, the problem is you. It is not your family members." I did not quarrel with him because he was right. I was the problem. I could not make my family members spend a whole day with mom. I was the only person whom I could change. Mom was not going to die if I took at least one day a week to relax.

Recently, I have started to take at least one day a week for myself. On that day, I unplug my telephone, and I make sure that I have uninterrupted time to do what invigorates me: my writing. The whole world could be falling apart, but if I have written, I am happy despite the hardships. On the other hand, if I have not written, no matter how wonderful the day is, it is not full, complete; it lacks the spark that makes me look forward to the next day. Therefore, no matter where you are in your life, you need to take time to be with yourself so that you can put energy into doing and being whatever it is that is authentically you. It's all right if your father wants to go into business for himself. But what do you want to do with *your* life? The only way to discover this is to spend time with yourself, putting energy into whatever invigorates you. If you do not spend quality time with yourself, you will never know happiness, which the world can never give, because happiness originates inside you. If this were not true, then why is it that two individuals can listen to the same piece of music, and one hates the piece and the other loves it? Just as you know what you love, you also know what will make you happy by furthering your life. The only way to do this is to take time, even if it is one day out of each week, to work on your passion; therefore, do not allow anyone to take these precious moments away from you. If you give this up, you have not realized your worth. You are not even important enough to spend time with yourself.

You may be in a situation where it is hard to imagine yourself finding peace and joy. You may feel overwhelmed with responsibilities. It seems as if you are not giving time and energy to your job, you have a spouse, family, or maybe a newborn infant who requires most of your care and attention. As a result, you neglect your needs. When we do this, we become angry at the very people whom we care about. In our overwhelmed state, we can reach the verge of a nervous breakdown. This is not the way to obtain happiness. Therefore, to bring more peace, joy, and ecstasy into your life, it is imperative that you take time out for yourself. At first, this may feel like it is going against your nature, especially if you have a propensity to give to others. But if you don't take responsibility for your happiness, then you eventually hurt those you love. If you are unhappy or overwhelmed, others will receive the brunt of your frustration. Usually, when we do not have time for ourselves, we are taking on too much. Often we take on the responsibilities of other people. When we do this, they do not grow, and neither do we. Therefore, we need to allow others to take responsibility for the problems they create. This will free up time for us, and it will give us a sense of freedom. One of the things that make people happy is their freedom, their ability to do what they want, what they enjoy. If we are constantly taking on responsibilities that belong to other people, we will never be happy. It is all right to help people with their problems, but do not take on the full responsibility as if the problem is yours. When we let other people solve the problems they create, they feel powerful because of their accomplishment, and we gain time and freedom to do the things we really love; it could be fishing, cooking, teaching, spending time with the kids, or whatever exhilarates us.

Also, we can give more time to ourselves by cutting back on, and even eliminating, tasks or activities that we can do without in order to put more energy into activities we enjoy. For example, instead of staying up to watch late night talk shows or to gorge on Hollywood gossip, go to bed early so that you can get up earlier to have more time for yourself. After all, talk shows are not going to create a life for you. The people on them are making their millions and are enjoying the good life, while you are scraping just to pay the bills.

Gregory F. Bearstop

Once you have set aside a few hours a week for yourself, you are ready to take the fourth step of expanding your vision of happiness: initially to use the time you set aside to begin to visualize ways of bringing more peace, joy, and ecstasy into your life.

Imagination is seeing with your third eye. It is visualizing what you cannot yet physically see. Everyone has an imagination, the ability to create in your mind. If something can happen in your mind, it can happen in your life. Everything that you can physically see began in someone's mind. This book, a television, a window, anything invented started as an idea in someone's mind. The first person to watch television was the inventor who initially watched it in his mind. If we can create marvelous things in our minds like the computer Internet, Nintendo, car phones, all the amenities we now enjoy, we can also begin to create in our minds a way that we can have more peace, joy, and happiness in our lives. Remember, if you don't first imagine your own happiness, you will never have it.

Visualizing can be fun because it is different from the way that our society encourages us to think. From an early age, we have been conditioned to visualize a traditional formula for happiness that can be monotonous, mundane, and devoid of creativity. We have been told that once you finish college, you get a job making a lucrative salary, have a family, and, when you retire, enjoy the rest of your life. This formula is what most people follow; yet, it does not work. It may have worked in the 1950s, 1960s, and early 1970s, when you could support a family on one parent's salary, but not today. Now the average income is not enough to support a family, send kids to college, and retire on; therefore, you spend most of your life killing yourself just to live, rather than living the life of joy that you could have. Begin to change your old pattern of visualizing a life that goes nowhere. There is a slogan that says, "If nothing changes, nothing changes." Therefore, if you want a happier life, you can have it by first picturing or visualizing it. To do this, you need to exercise your creative powers.

First, commence your visualization process by becoming comfortable with being creative. This is the key to visualizing, because if you are not comfortable with creating, your ideas will never get off the ground; you will chalk them up as ludicrous, stupid, and not worth pursuing. You will psyche yourself out of creating a better life. Thus to create, you need to open up the whole universe before you. Place yourself in the field of infinite possibilities. In order to do this, you need to come up with things that you can do to put yourself in a creative mood. These are activities or ways of thinking that will free you to let go of the restraints that block your creative energy. Remember to use only the ideas that will totally relax you to let yourself go. Apply this before you start your visualization process. When you do this, some of the most wonderful, fascinating ideas will spontaneously flow out of you. Here are some ideas or activities that can free you so that you can begin to visualize ways of bringing more peace and joy into your life:

1. All thoughts or ideas are valid.
2. All thoughts or ideas can be changed.
3. Recall a challenging situation that resulted in a successful outcome. Relive this experience in your mind until you start to feel relaxed and confident.
4. Feed yourself a diet of authors, writers, or artists who inspire you.

5. Do a meditation exercise that induces relaxation
6. Listen to inspiring music.

If you have some of your own ideas or activities that help you to loosen up, please add them to this list.

Once you are in a creative mood, you are ready to take the next step in the visualization process: to picture the one thing that you really love doing. This is something that gives you the most joy, your passion, and it is a positive influence for you to become your best self. To find out what your passion is, ask yourself: If there was something positive that I could be doing every day that gives me the most joy, what would I be doing? There may be several activities or endeavors that come to mind. Pick the one that exhilarates you the most, one that you can actually see yourself doing. Begin to visualize it. See yourself going through each step. Visualize in color because this makes the experience more real. See the results of doing this activity. Allow yourself to feel the joy associated with it.

The fifth step in expanding our vision of our own happiness is to take the activity that you enjoy the most and begin to brainstorm ways that you can improve it and put it into the service of humanity. This is a significant quality of every person who truly experiences success. Look at a great star like Michael Jordan. In high school, he couldn't make the varsity team; however, because of his love for basketball and his willingness to stay after school to practice with his coach, he has become a renowned basketball legend. At the same time, much of his success is due to his willingness to place his love for basketball at the service of humanity. He has helped to give humanity an enjoyment for basketball through the caliber and unique style in which he plays the game. What Michael Jordan has done for basketball, we can do for endeavors that ignite our passion.

There are several ways of improving what you love doing. For instance, if you enjoy writing songs, then you may see yourself perfecting this skill by taking a course in music composition, spending a few hours a day learning how to play your favorite instrument, spending time composing and modifying a piece of music, and so on. List ways that you can begin to develop your passion. Begin to see in detail, step by step, what you need to do in order to develop your passion and have others benefit from it. It is important that you often visualize the first thing that you need to do and play the whole process out in your mind until you are pleased with the excellence that you have produced. Now you are building momentum that will naturally propel you to take the first step toward improving your special talent. Here are some ways to do this:

1. Learn all that you can about the area you want to develop. Les Brown, the motivational speaker, says become a student of the area in which you are interested. Here are two ways to do this:

    a. Take courses ranging from introductory to advanced courses in this field.
    b. Read books featuring people who have successfully accomplished goals that you wish to achieve.

2. Don't just drop everything and run out to try to accomplish your goal overnight. Take the little steps that will move you toward mastering what you love to do.

3. Communicate and interact with people who have made great strides in your field.

   a. Speak with someone who has accomplished what you aim to do, and find out how they achieved this goal. Their wisdom will be the instructions you can follow, of course with some degree of flexibility.

   b. Surround yourself with successful people, because the more you interact with them, the more you will take on the thinking patterns and behaviors needed to master your passion.

4. Learn and use new words as often as you can, because when you do this, you expand your world of ideas, which leads to new discoveries. It is when you discover new and innovative ways of doing something you love that you become the best at what you do.

5. Read poetry, mythologies, and science fiction literature; this is another powerful strategy for perfecting your passion. Whereas expanding your vocabulary helps to increase your ability to think of new ideas, reading poetry, mythologies, and science fiction stimulates you to put ideas together, thus embarking upon new discoveries. Now you think what-if, instead of just sticking to what is. Now your creative juices start to flow.

6. Listen to your intuition about how to become the best at what you love doing. Trust your instincts, because you are inextricably connected to a universal force that knows the best course of action to take. If you trust it, it will undoubtedly lead you to where you want to go.

As I began to develop my communication skills, I became very interested in public speaking. When I began delivering speeches, I was notorious for stumbling over words and not finishing a complete thought. But I continued to learn from my mistakes and practice good oratory skills. I studied and tried to emulate great speakers. I would incorporate different aspects of these styles into my own. I watched segments of Dr. Martin Luther King, Jr.'s most famous speeches, and I noted how he magnetized vast audiences. I felt the electricity that his speeches so acutely evoked. He would set me on fire. I would read poetry to exercise my imagination so that I could present ordinary ideas in a new and lively manner. I also read the dictionary to increase my means for communicating with a variety of people. As I used these strategies, I became a better speaker.

I now deliver speeches that inspire and help people to transcend the obstacles that block their path to a more passionate life.

Several months ago, I delivered the eulogy at a relative's funeral. Afterward, several people stopped me to say that they were so moved that they wanted me to do the eulogy at their funerals. I responded by asking them, when did they plan on dying?

You cannot lose when you live out your passion and put it at the service of others. When you enjoy what you do, you want to perfect it, produce the best quality. When you have the best quality and you begin to enhance the lives of other people with it, they will reward you with abundant resources. This is why you will never make as much money doing something you have very little interest in. Money is a by-product of perfecting the endeavor that you really love doing and putting it at the service of others. Therefore, not only will you feel good having the means to obtain the things that make life a little more comfortable, such as a car or a nice home, but most important, you will have a sense of fulfillment that comes from knowing that other people's lives are a little better because of something that you have perfected. This is most important, because your car or home can be stolen or destroyed, but the fulfillment that comes from improving the lives of other people can never be taken away from you.

CHAPTER 4

EXPAND YOUR VISION OF WHO YOU ARE AND WHAT YOU ARE CAPABLE OF DOING

Many of us do not see our true potential; we really do not know what we are capable of doing. Many of us are stuck in jobs where we are unhappy. We feel like we are not fully utilizing our talents and unique abilities. We do not feel challenged to become a master of the skills we possess. Some of us are in relationships where we are not growing and experiencing life. One main reason why so many people are unhappy, which in turn affects their relationships, is because they are not doing something positive that they really love. This is where greatness is manifested. Everyone has a talent to do something better than anyone else. They do this in such a way that no one else will be able to imitate it. You do not realize your greatness, how well you do something, by doing things that you are not really interested in or don't really enjoy. Most of us spend our energy and time doing a lot of things adequately. In fact, we may do these tasks quite well. We do a proficient job at work. Our chores and hobbies are no obstacles. But you don't feel good or special by doing ordinary things in a satisfactory manner. You are going to feel special by mastering an endeavor that you really love doing. This will not feel like a labor-intense task. In fact, it will feel spontaneous and natural. Doing what you love is not work. The more you engage in this activity, the better you will become at it.

If you do not have passion for something, it is not likely that you will become a master of it. When you do not develop your particular gift or talent, then you do not fully experience and feel your greatness and worth. Yet feeling your own greatness, your incalculable worth, is the fuel that will lead you not only to make your life better but also to better the lives of others by putting your talents at the service of humanity.

When you do not develop your skills or particular talent, you become comfortable with being mediocre. No one gets excited about being mediocre. This is nothing to write home about. You don't feel your own value when you settle for mediocrity. In fact, the *Winston Dictionary* defines mediocre as "having only a moderate degree of worth." Feeling mediocre is not going to give you the energy to make wonderful things happen in your life. But you can change this feeling by listening to your inner voice which tells you to do what you really love. When you do this, you will automatically want to develop your particular talent. Because of your passion for this activity, you've got to find out more. You begin to learn skills and techniques that have made others a master of this endeavor. Out of interest, you want to see whether these techniques can improve your abilities. Deep down, you know that the better you become, the more enjoyment you are likely to have. By trying these techniques and adapting them to your own style, you notice improvement that gets you excited to the point where you want to develop your skills further. As you continue to learn new techniques and improve, you will eventually master this skill. During the process, you will feel good about yourself; you will feel your greatness and value more acutely. This is something to write home about. You will feel good within yourself because you will be pleased with your own works. When you feel inflated, in touch with your own greatness and worth, you have power.

Happiness That Is Guaranteed

The way to expand your vision of who you really are, to realize your greatness, is to take the pressure off yourself. Quite simply, give yourself a break. In fact, take a lifelong vacation from pulverizing and beating yourself up. We put too much pressure on ourselves. We seem to remind ourselves constantly about all the things that we should have done. There is nothing wrong with taking care of our obligations and responsibilities; however, some of us take on too much. Furthermore, no one likes to be told what to do. We don't even like telling *ourselves* what to do. Usually we end up doing the opposite, or we conveniently avoid doing what we should. Therefore, the way to begin to expand your vision of who you really are, to realize your greatness, is by accepting who you are at this moment. If you have not accomplished the things that you want to, it is all right. You may be angry or hurt because of some situation. Your parents may have divorced. You may have lost a child or a loved one. No matter what your disappointments or present situation may be, accept it. Don't apologize for it. Instead, proclaim it confidently as where you are right now. I remember that a client in treatment for alcohol dependence said to me, "I don't care what you say to me; I am going to have my two or three beers in the evening when I come home from a hard day of work." I was struck by the truthfulness of this statement. The client may not have been facing the reality of the inevitable negative consequences of his drinking, but he was being honest about what was happening at that moment. However, the problem that keeps many people from realizing their greatness is that they do not accept all the good that they are and have accomplished. This is what it means to accept all of you, the good with the bad. But most of us augment the difficulties to the extent of overshadowing the wonderful things about us. Our accomplishments are the fuel that will lead us to become our best self and cause even more wonderful things to happen in our lives. For the most part, we are not motivated to take positive action by dwelling on the things that make us feel bad, things that cause us to devalue ourselves.

I remember a ten-year-old boy who was learning karate. He did not show an exceptional talent for this art; in fact, he was sought of awkward. But one day he discovered that his favorite kick was the sidekick. He enjoyed practicing it. He enjoyed it so much that every day he would work on improving a different part of the kick until it was perfect. He felt so good that he had perfected one aspect that he began improving another aspect of his sidekick. The better he became, the more he loved his sidekick. In two months, he went from having an awkward diffident sidekick to winning a trophy for the most outstanding student for the month of November. This is an excellent example of how focusing on the little insignificant accomplishments can not only motivate us to take positive action but can also cause wonderful things to happen.

Remember that the key to progress and realizing your greatness is focusing on and doing things that affirm your incalculable worth. Not only do we need to draw upon our past and present accomplishments, but we need to affirm our value as a human being. If nothing that I have done causes me to feel good about myself, I still have value. Even if I were paralyzed, I still have ineffable value as a human being, a person who is a gift from God to the world. I am a being who has life. You cannot say that life itself has no value. If I do this, I also deny the reality that a beautiful sunrise, an oceanic view, and a mountainous vista have value even though they are powerful enough to cause me to feel calm, tranquility, and awe. If they can do this, they certainly do have meaning and value. These things either come from life or are a part of it. If they have value, the life in you is certainly valuable. Therefore, realizing that you have value as a unique person who has a reason for being here, you can use the energy generated from feeling your worth to help you to obtain what you desire out of life.

To feel your own worth consistently, it is essential that you do something good for yourself. Treat yourself to dinner at a good restaurant. Take a few extra hours to catch up on sleep, or do something restful. Prepare a refreshing bubble bath for yourself. When you take time out to do nice things for yourself, you are giving yourself the message that you are valuable, and, as a result, you will feel better about yourself. I emphasize this because you will not obtain the happiness you want if you do not feel good about yourself. Your happiness starts at home, within you.

Everyone has a purpose in this life. It is a purpose that no one else can fulfill in the unique way that only you can. At the same time, it is something that you really love to do and that you can put into the service of humanity. By doing so, you can experience even more satisfaction by knowing that you are doing your part in furthering the advancement of humanity. However, if you do not fulfill your purpose, you will never be as happy as you could. Your purpose in life is inextricably connected to your happiness. A person who gets a lot of joy out of being a social worker is not going to be happy as a computer technician (which he might become simply to make a living). Thus a key to your happiness is living your passion. Once you find what that is, then you must begin to find a way to make it a reality in your life. This is where your greatness lies. In order to find a way to do what you really love, it is essential that you tap into and maintain the flow of energy that moves you toward accomplishing your goals and becoming the best person that you can. You are also motivated to act in the interest of your happiness by living in your mind the negative, undesirable consequence of not taking action to increase your own sense of fulfillment. The key to unlocking your greatness, who you really are, is feeling your worth, having self-appreciation, self-love that leads you to value others.

THE POWER WITHIN YOU

Four years ago in southeast Washington, D.C., I was helping clients to overcome their addictions and to maintain a sober life-style. It was then that I really began to question whether I was happy. I enjoyed my job, but I was not happy. I did not like the drive to work along streets lined with rundown buildings and people who seemed to make a career out of hanging on the corners. I felt constantly frustrated and (at times) depressed because, although I was providing a good service, I did not feel that I was where I was supposed to be. However, deep inside, I had a nagging feeling that I would find happiness, or at least a better life, in Toronto, Canada. I had always loved this city because I felt that the people were kinder than the people in most other cities. I was in awe of the city's beauty depicted in the street cars, coffee shops, the architectural layout of its buildings, the multicultural influences, the city's emphasis on protecting the environment, and a host of other attractions. Besides, I felt that I would find my future wife there. But the obstacle that stood in the way of realizing this dream was that I was settled in Washington, DC.

On September 26, 1994, my frustration, depression, and overall discontent had reached such an intense level that I

Happiness That Is Guaranteed

saw only one way out. On that day, I quit my job. I packed all my necessary belongings, I loaded my car and I drove 600 miles to Toronto. At last, I thought, I was free, and my days of happiness had begun.

I stayed in Toronto for about a month and a half. I spent most of my time looking for employment. I thoroughly enjoyed the night life, movies, dancing, and socializing with new friends. It was an adventure in which each day brought something new, unexpected, and exciting.

However, about a month later, reality began to set in. Nobody would hire me because I did not have a work visa. I could not find a job where the employer was pressed to hire me over a Canadian who could do the job just as well. The people did not seem as exceptionally kind as I once believed. It was true that no place has a monopoly on kind people; there are good and bad people everywhere. While I began to discover that not everything in Toronto was going to appeal to me, I also realized that there were many things that I enjoyed. I experienced some happy moments and some disappointments. As it became more evident that I needed to return to Washington, D.C., because of my lack of success in finding employment, I realized that happiness does not come from being in a particular place. A city, town, or country cannot give me happiness. These places can contribute to good times and elicit pleasurable feelings, but they cannot give me peace and a feeling of completeness. I discovered this while sitting in a lounge on the 51st floor of Toronto's Manual Life Building overlooking a breathtaking panoramic view of the city at night. Instead of being in awe, I felt painfully lonely; I was still not happy, even when I was surrounded by so much beauty.

Gregory F. Bearstop

Upon my return to Washington, D.C., I felt better than when I left. Living in Toronto was a dream that I needed to get out of my system. I did not regret quitting my job to experience this, because if I had not done so, I would have always wondered what would have happened. Now I know, and I was ready to continue my search for happiness.

Two weeks after I returned, I attended a seminar given by a trainee of Anthony Robbins, the author of two best-seller books, "Unlimited Power" and "Unleashing the Giant Within." This was the best seminar that I had ever attended. The theme was about getting people to believe that they could achieve their dreams if they took action to make them a reality. The facilitator introduced you to some exercises in which you were instructed to picture your life ten years from now. You were guided to visualize what your life would be like, first, if you neglected to act on your dreams, and second, if you took action and accomplished your dreams.

By midafternoon, the seminar reached a dramatic climax when your belief and confidence in yourself were challenged. You were given the task of breaking an 8 1/2"x 11" board with your bare hands. It was evident from the quiet and somber mood in the room that many of us had doubts about breaking the board.

Initially, I did not think that I could break the board. I kept examining my board for signs of weakness, but there were none. I remembered that in karate school, you would have to train for two years before you broke boards, and here I was supposed to break a board with only ten minutes of instruction.

When the time came to break my board, my coach guided me to look past my fear of failure and to picture the fulfillment of my dreams on the other side of the board.

Happiness That Is Guaranteed

The more I focused on the other side with energy, determination, and strength, the more I believed that it was possible. On the count of three, I struck the board. Instantly, the sound of breaking through rang out. I broke through to the other side!

After celebrating, I felt like a new person. I believed that I could accomplish any goal. It was like I had stumbled upon a small door to happiness and I had found one of several keys to unlocking it. For the first time in my life I knew what it was like to feel whole; I knew what it was like to be truly happy. A light was turned on inside me. Feeling that I could accomplish anything, I rushed home to change my life. I asked myself: If there was something that I could be doing every day that would give me the most joy, what would it be? After doing some soul-searching, I felt that if I could help at least one person to find happiness in his or her life, that would give me the greatest joy. If I did this, they could bury me in my grave and I would be fine. Later in the night, I was led to write a book about finding happiness that would allow me to influence even more people. That is how this book came into being.

The elation that I felt from breaking the board made me realize more than anything else that happiness really does not come from anything outside me, but from within. Now you may say that breaking the board, which is something outside you, made me happy. This may have been the catalyst; however, breaking the board cannot sustain happiness. Only your beliefs and attitude inside you can sustain happiness. Remember that happiness is having the assurance that everything is going to be all right. That assurance comes from connecting with things inside you that last, such as inner strength; love; and those virtues, beliefs, and attitudes that promote love. There is nothing that you can plug into outside yourself that is going to make you happy. Why? Because you can't control those things. One minute, they are fulfilling. Another minute, they're an addiction; they are an enslavement. They change. They get old like our possessions. They wear out. They can be destroyed. They can leave us. They do not guarantee our happiness. They do not last. Therefore, if we are going to be happy, we are going to find it within ourselves. Inside! Inside! Inside!

Many authors have written extensively on how to obtain happiness. They tell you that happiness is freeing yourself from certain things, obtaining peace or fulfillment. We understand much of what they are saying. Their message rings true, but it doesn't seem to be personalized. It is not personalized because these authors need to be more concrete. Earlier, we said that happiness is a feeling or sense of peace, fulfillment, and completeness that comes from knowing that everything is going to be all right. Now let's take the first part about fulfillment and completeness. These concepts are too abstract. They need to be broken down so that we can put our hands on them. So far in this book, we have done just that. We have begun to see fulfillment concretely and specifically as pursuing a positive life-giving endeavor that gives you the most joy and putting it at the service of others. However, this is only one part of fulfillment. The other part comes from feeling that everything is going to be all right. How does a person arrive at this feeling? We have begun to address this when we have talked about situations that involve inner strength. These were times when you may have been in a hopeless situation. Others doubted your abilities. The outcome looked bleak and unpleasant. Yet, there was an inner power or presence that told you to keep going; you can do it.

Happiness That Is Guaranteed

Despite what most people thought, you made it through incredible odds intact. This was the same inner power that led me to break the board at the seminar. When you are plugged into your inner power, you can confront and surpass any challenge. This is possible because on an unconscious level, your inner power has given you the assurance that everything is going to be all right even if there are difficult risks to take. Otherwise, if you did not feel this assurance, you could not accomplish even the smallest challenges because you would not have the strength and initiative to do so. This is why there are people dying of cancer and other illnesses who are happy and totally at peace. They are in touch with the assurance of their inner power. Even if they should die, it is going to be all right. They may feel that they are going to be in a better place and their suffering will end, or they may have a host of other comforting thoughts. But the strength of these individuals could conquer armies. They are so strong that even a deadly disease could not rob them of their happiness. When you access your inner power, you will always have a foundation of peace, fulfillment, and completeness. But before we can access it, we need to know what is this power within us. Let's take a closer look.

Chapter 5

Expand Your Vision of the Power Within You

Once you begin to exercise self-love and to feel your own worth, it is essential that you expand your vision of the power within you. If you don't, you run the risk of abusing this power, your greatest resource. Often we do not work in harmony with our power if we are unaware of what it is.

One way of recognizing this power is by watching a person charged with energy. In some ways, what is even more impressive is recognizing power within yourself. It can be displayed on many occasions. For instance, suppose that you are in a cashier line and someone enters the line in front of you. You alert the person that you were in line before him; however, he insists that you are mistaken. You begin to argue. You are yelling at each other. You begin to sweat. Both of you become so enraged that you feel like doing violence to each other. He hits you. At this point, you defend yourself. Clothes are being torn. Things are being knocked over. You come at him like a steam engine, punching, kicking, smashing until security guards pull you apart. To a bystander, he or she would be amazed at the incredible energy and power that exploded in you.

Not only does anger release tremendous energy within us, but on the other side of the spectrum, love also demonstrates our power. When you fall in love, your power is displayed in the many caring and compassionate acts that you do for your lover.

As you can see, the power within us is manifested in many ways, especially through our emotions and feelings. To some degree, we know what it is like to feel anger, love, frustration, disappointment, and so on. But, do we know what these feelings are? We know what they feel like. But do we really know what we are dealing with?

First, we cannot see these feelings. We cannot physically see anger or love itself. We cannot see it, smell it, taste it, or touch it. Feelings do not have a particular shape or form. You cannot pick love up and put it on the table. Feelings are immaterial.

Second, since feelings are immaterial, having no physical shape or form, they do not have boundaries. Therefore, feelings such as anger or love cannot be confined to any particular person or place; instead, they can spread on forever. Anger can spread rapidly through a crowd and a nation (as we saw in the Los Angeles riots of 1993). Love can also spread throughout crowds (as was demonstrated when Nelson Mandela came to America soon after his release from twenty years of imprisonment; the love and admiration for this man were evident in the jubilation of the crowds that met him). Thus the power of our feelings cannot be confined by boundaries. Instead, it is free to go wherever it wishes. It is not bound by time and space. Feelings do not discriminate from one culture to another. This is why just as a white man or woman can feel hatred for a black man or woman and visa versa, a white man or woman can also love a black man or woman and visa versa.

Third, feelings have the power to move. They can move people to act in certain ways. When you are angry, often you are moved to express it verbally or to do violence. Likewise, when you are moved by love, you express it through words, giftgiving, affection, hugs, kisses, and so on. Our feelings are always moving us to act the way we do.

Fourth, because feelings have no shape or form, have no limits, and can move people to act, they are in the spiritual realm. An entity that has no shape or form, has no limits, and can produce action or movement is spirit. Therefore, feelings are spiritual.

Sometimes after people visit their sick relative in the hospital, they report that their relative's "spirits" were up. By this, they are saying that their relative was feeling better or cheerful. Here again, feelings are identified as spirit. Since we have feelings in us and feelings are spiritual, then we have spirit within us. If you have ever watched a person sing a song so passionately that it moves you to tears, you have witnessed the spirit within this singer. What is this passion? It is intangible and has no limits. It is so powerful that it can move and inspire an audience of millions. This passion is of the spirit. The spirit is real. Because if it were not, you would not have been inspired or moved to tears. The song could have been sung in a monotone voice, very staid and bleak. A robot could have done as much.

Some people do not want to talk about or have anything to do with spirit. They become anxious and fearful. This happens because of some of the things they associate with spirit. Many people associate the term "spirit" with religion; however, spirit is not religion. Religion is the way one lives out his or her beliefs or convictions. Therefore, when we speak of spirit, we are not talking about anybody's religion at all. When we use the term "spirit," we are referring to an aspect of all of us that moves us to act.

Earlier we mentioned that our feelings are one way of displaying the power within us. Feelings, being in the spiritual realm, have the capacity to move us to act, for spirit is the impetus that produces movement within us. In

Happiness That Is Guaranteed

order to produce movement, we need energy or power. Nothing moves or acts without a source of power.

To see how the spirit supplies us with constant power, let's try a little exercise. Take a moment, and place your hand over your heart. Feel and listen to your heart beating. This happens 24 hours a day, 365 days a year. Take another moment and listen to your breathing, the constant inhaling and exhaling of oxygen. Consider the hundreds of times this is done daily. What are the basic sources that keep us breathing and keeps our heart beating? Initially, some of us may conclude that the intake of oxygen and our constant blood flow maintain our breathing and pulse. Although this is true, it is only part of the life-sustaining process. Oxygen and blood are essential components for life, but when we analyze the process further, we will discover prominent sources that provide the impetus and power for carrying out these vital functions. To help us identify these sources, let us consider the automobile, because it seems to use energy sources in much of the same way we do.

When asked to name sources of energy that the automobile requires, one source that comes to mind is gasoline or fuel. But in order to burn fuel, your car needs an initial spark or boost to set the process into motion. This spark occurs when the energy from the battery is released. Thus the battery is a major source of energy for your car.

When we look at the major sources involved in our car's functioning, we will discover that the fundamental mechanical concept for supplying power to our car is based upon the human body and how it receives energy to keep it alive. Just as the automobile requires fuel to burn, thus producing power, the human body needs food that is metabolized to give our bodies energy. Food is the fuel of our bodies; however, recall that fuel is not the only essential source of power for the automobile—but the battery is equally important. Therefore, in applying this simile to the human body, I will ask this question: What is it that acts as the battery of the human being? Like a battery, we have energy flowing through us. This power, exhibited through our feelings and thoughts (which are immaterial, limitless, and move us), is spirit. Only spirit can supply power to things that are immaterial and have no boundaries, such as our feelings and thoughts. Material things such as fuel, food, etc., cannot give power to things that are immaterial and have no boundaries. Material things are too limited. This is why the battery of the human being is spirit. It enlivens our bodies, enabling us to move about and produce actions. It is the life that is in us. All of us have spirit within us; otherwise, we could not function, we could not live. To keep our spirit going, we need power. We do not have batteries attached to us. We, unlike huge generators, are not powered by mighty rivers or by water, wind, or fuel. Our power is our spirit.

When a battery's energy is consumed, it needs recharging. We also need recharging. How often have you heard someone say: "I need a vacation. I need a revival. I need rejuvenating." These statements express a need for more energy and power. In order for the spirit to reenergized us, we need a power that is constant and does not run out. If this power was not provided at any given moment, all of us would cease to be. Therefore, the spirit's power has to be constant. But how does this happen?

In order for the spirit to give us constant power, there must be an entity in the universe that is nothing but pure power. This power does not lack anything within itself. It has no boundaries. It is freedom. Only pure power can give power to something that is endless and has no limits, such

Happiness That Is Guaranteed

as our spirit. This power, which has no limits and can sustain the endless, is God. Only God does not need anything and can give power to spirit. If God could not do this, He could not be God. If there were a lack or deficiency within God, then God could not sustain spirit. Eventually spirit would die; instantly, this would be the end of all life.

As a side note, to be true to God, who is without limits, from this point onward, I will not identify God as only masculine. Instead, I will identify God as masculine in this chapter and as feminine in the next chapter. I will continue to alternate between referring to God as masculine and feminine from chapter to chapter. I will do this as a way of being true to who God is: a being who is without limits. Because of this, God is manifested to the world not only through masculinity but also through feminity.

Although God has been described in many ways, what we are concerned about right now is God as Pure Power. But we are not easily convinced that we need God. Earlier we mentioned that each person's spirit has no limits. If this is so, then isn't our spirit capable of sustaining us by itself? While our spirit has no limits, on another level, it does lack something in and of itself. Doesn't this sound like a contradiction? However, it is not a contradiction when we look at the whole picture. Our spirit lacks. This is what we experience when we feel empty inside. We want something to fill the emptiness, to complete us, to fulfill us. God can complete our spirit, because God does not lack anything. This God is also Spirit, because only a being or entity that has no shape and is endless in itself can sustain and support another entity that is limitless. It is like a cup made to carry an ounce of water cannot hold a gallon, but a cup capable of carrying a gallon of water can hold an ounce or a gallon. The reality is that all of us have spirit. We have thoughts and feelings, which are spirit. Our spirit empowers and enlivens us. It is sustained and it receives its potency from Pure Power, which is God. Therefore, this God, in and through our spirit, gives us life and maintains it. The only way that we can join with God is through our spirit. This is why our spirit is the most direct channel to God. Without it, we could not connect with God. He is too far beyond us. He is infinite, having no limits, endless. We are finite, having very pronounced limits. If we did not have spirit, then we would never be fulfilled. The story of our journey toward fulfillment, our spiritual journey, reaches a dramatic climax in the actual joining or coming together of our spirit and the Spirit of God. The only reason why this union happens is because God is Love itself. And Love is constantly drawing people together and maintaining their harmonious union. It holds the planets in their orbits and keeps the universe at one with itself. If it were not for Love itself, our spirit and God would never be drawn together. Because God is Love that can never end, unconditional love, God can satisfy our spirit. You don't have to believe in God. God exists whether you believe in Him or not. But if you have treated someone charitably or if you had this done to you, then you have experienced God. The caring or love itself is God. God's power flows in a cyclical pattern. When a person experiences God, when they experience being cared for in such a way that they know within their heart that the love will never end, they are so fulfilled that they cannot help but share it with others. Love goes around. It spreads. Just as a circle is round and never ends, so is the pattern of life within us.

There is nothing that can outdo the experience of love that does not end, love that is unconditional. This is why God being Love itself is the greatest of all things. So what about death? Can death destroy love? If two people genuinely love each other and one dies, is the love that the deceased person felt destroyed? Death is the demise of the material, the body; therefore, the love that the deceased person felt cannot be destroyed. It's not physical or material. Thus love lives on. Love is spirit. And spirit cannot die unless it is separated from God.

Therefore, this discussion boils down to three points. The first point is that God is real. God is a real being or presence. If God is not real, then you and I would not be here right now. Many people picture God as a force that is not conscious. He just draws things together because that's what His nature is. He has no thoughts. He is not conscious of what He is doing. This is the mentality of a lot of people. This is the way we live in today's society. We live like God isn't conscious of what we are doing, isn't conscious of us and our needs, and, in His consciousness doesn't want to communicate with us even better than we could with our best friend. Nothing could be further from the truth. If God were just a force out there, an energy source of love with no intelligence, not able to communicate with us, then God would be lacking. Remember that God does not lack anything, not even the ability to communicate with you on an intimate level. Because if He did, He could not be God. Therefore, God is a concerned being, a real personality.

The second point is that God is the power within you. The power within you that is manifested through thought and feelings is spirit. And because spirit is empowered by God, God is enlivening the spirit. This is possible because our spirit has no limits, and therefore it can join with God, who is beyond limits. Since spirit is within us and receives its power from God, then God is the power that is within us.

Gregory F. Bearstop

One of the best ways to discover the power within you is through some challenging situation or crisis. It is amazing how crisis can bring out the best in people. They muster up inner strength that they did not know they had.

There are many elements that enable you to overcome trials, but there is one element that makes all the difference. It is the power and energy within you that pursue life unceasingly. In looking back over your crises, it was the unswerving force that would not allow you to be overtaken. It would not allow you to lose hope and die. Instead, like a mighty gale it raised you and carried you with unshakable force through unforeseen chaos to a place of soothing tranquility. Even when you put yourself down, it is the power that keeps you going. It says to you: "Get up. Do not listen to what other people are saying. I know that you can do it!"

For example, suppose that you are paralyzed from the waist down with partial paralysis in your arms after being involved in a serious car accident. Your four closest friends, who were in the car with you and were not hospitalized for any serious injuries, never visited you in the hospital. A month later, your spouse comes to the hospital with divorce papers and an insurance policy. You are horrified, especially because one of the things you valued most, your marriage, is disintegrating. Besides, you do not feel that anyone else will marry you, especially now that you are paralyzed. How do you survive this ordeal? How do you begin to build a life for yourself after you have lost so much?

This is a devastating experience. I do not know what I would do. You may share my sentiment. Nonetheless, you or I would have to deal with it. At some point, you would have to get in touch with some power or force to survive the mental anxiety and the physical and emotional pain. When severe pain persists for hours and you are emotionally fatigued, only a sustaining power, that inner drive for life, can carry you through times when your survival is in question. It was this sustaining power that enabled President Nelson Mandela to endure imprisonment for justice and to emerge twenty years later stronger than he ever was. This is the same power, soul force, that has enabled you to overcome your most menacing trials to bring you to this moment.

The example of paralysis is based on a true story of a dear friend who continues to deal courageously with her condition. Her inner power has carried her through much pain and anxiety. She left the hospital and is living in her home which is designed to meet her challenges. Her positive spirit enables her to continue enjoying many activities such as attending movies, classes, and socials. Her life is a testament to the sustaining power which we all embody.

When we draw upon the power of God within us, we will deal more effectively with our trials and we will be confident and strong enough to overcome any crisis. This is where lasting happiness comes from. Remember that happiness is the fulfillment that comes from feeling that everything is going to be all right. We mentioned earlier that fulfillment is doing whatever it is that you really love to do, pursuing your passion. But we really never nailed down the second part: how do I feel the assurance that everything is going to be all right on a consistent basis?

This brings us to our third point: you and I can feel that everything is going to be all right by being in touch with, connected with, and in relationship with God, who lacks nothing. This sounds so simple, so elementary, why should

I waste my time exploring this concept further? But for those who actually feel that God is taking care of them, come what may, this experience is ultimately profound. When I mention that with God everything will be all right, this does not mean that God does all the work. If I need a new job, I am going to have to go on interviews, put in applications, and do everything in my power to obtain employment. However, at the same time, if I am in relationship with God, who sees my efforts, He will supply all else that is needed to attain my goal. You will never feel that everything is going to be all right if you are not connected with God, who lacks nothing. Because God is within you, when you are connected with God and in relationship with God, you will also feel what it is like to lack nothing. When you do not want for anything, how can things not be all right, how can they not turn out in a positive light? This is true peace, true happiness. Nothing can crush me. Nothing can keep me down. Nothing can have the final word.

Now it's great to talk about getting in touch with God, but the reality is that we allow many things, especially feelings and beliefs, to prevent us from connecting with Him. In order for us to experience God, lasting happiness, at some point, we have to face the obstacles that keep us denying the reality of His presence and how awesome our lives can be when we experience the fruits of not lacking anything.

CHAPTER 6

WHAT IS BLOCKING YOU FROM YOUR INNER POWER?

For many of us, God is dead. We don't believe in God anymore. Good. Godlike people, compassionate people, and the mystics have all told us time and time again that God has to die in us in order for us to find God. They are really saying that in order for us to find the *true* God, the *false* God has to die. The false God is the one who stifles us and overwhelms us with all these rules that She uses to lord over us. We go to church because we *have* to, instead of because we *want* to. We may feel that if we don't attend church, God will see us as a bad person or someone who is undeserving of Her love. So we attend church out of fear of God's wrath, rather than because we want to share the joy of experiencing the true God of freedom and peace in community.

The true God is the caring loving presence within you. When everyone else gives up on you, it still believes in you. God, this loving presence, has no limits. Because of this, the true God frees you. It does not matter how many mistakes you have made or how much of a mess you've gotten yourself into, the true God is still there as the voice within you that says, "I still believe in you. With me, you can overcome any challenge." God frees us because She does not allow even the worst judgments we make about ourselves to separate us from Her. There is no limit to the love that God has for you. Even when we commit our worst mistakes, in our darkest moments, the true God is still reassuring us, believing in us. When you open up the channels to hearing Her voice and listen to Her, you will have power that will shake the world. When you really listen to God's reassuring voice, you will experience Her loving you without conditions, without limits. Then you will have a sense in you that you lack nothing. Who could lack anything when they feel within themselves love that has no end?

When you feel endless love within you, you will also feel tremendous power. This is why it is so important to get in touch with God by listening to Her voice and communicating with Her, because it is the power that comes out of this relationship that will enable you to accomplish your purpose in life, which is a significant part of your fulfillment. This is why it is important to get in touch with the true God. When you are working on a major goal, things will happen that will cause you to want to give up. This is why self-esteem and confidence alone are not enough. We are not always going to feel confident, self-assured. But when we are in touch with the true God, the power from this relationship will give us inner strength when we feel deficient.

Let me also say that if we do not get in touch with the true God, we have a greater risk of not having the sound judgment that we need in order to find our purpose in life, to choose dreams and goals that will be fulfilling. Hitler felt that his purpose in life was to secure the supremacy of the Aryan culture over all other cultures. But look what happened: it was not a dream based in sound judgment. It was not a dream based in a just consciousness. And it failed. If we do not care about how our decisions affect the lives of other people, then we are not in touch with God. If this is the case, we are not going to have sound judgment based on seeing the wider picture. My choices are based on my narrow world, which includes only me, instead of on a panoramic view of the real world, which includes me and everyone else. Without God, it is more difficult to have the consciousness that will enable you to more readily distinguish between goals that are fulfilling and those that will end in disaster.

There are so many people choosing dreams doomed to fail, dreams that are never going to give them fulfillment. And that is sad. Many of us have divorced God from our endeavors. Only a true God can give you a life of happiness. Again that does not mean that we don't do our part. If we do our part, God, who sees our good efforts, will bring our goals and dreams to fulfillment. And even if that does not happen, our happiness does not depend upon those goals and dreams, because being in relationship with God Herself is joy enough. With Her, there is nothing that we lack.

So you don't believe in God anymore. Good. Now you can begin to discover the *true* God. If you want to experience the most freedom and joy in your life, this is an opportunity to overcome or move beyond the obstacles that separate you from God and to recognize God as the power within you.

One of the first things that block us from getting in touch with God is the very concept of God. Even the word "God" is a block, because it conveys the idea of a being who is infinite, who is greater than us. We can't even conceive of what that is like. It can be mind-boggling. Because the concept of God is difficult to grasp, it can be very threatening to us. This is normal, very natural. We are not threatened by something that is not as great as we are. So even the concept of God can be a barrier, because it is scary to think about connecting with a being who has no end, who's infinite. And therefore, it can keep us at a distance, not wanting to venture and find out more. This is why to move beyond the concept, it is important that we *experience* God. The acceptance of the concept of God comes in the experience. Otherwise, we're looking at God from the sidelines as a spectator, but not as a participant. When we experience God, we can accept the concept more; however, we can't experience God if we are not able to deal with our blocks. This is why it is so important that we deal with these obstacles by becoming aware of them and by understanding how they are blocking us from a relationship with God.

By the way, not dealing with our blocks is what gets us into trouble. This is hell for us. Many people think that God sends people to hell. (This is part of the false image of God.) Hell is known to be a place that you deserve when you have done many evil things. It's a place that God sends you to punish you for all eternity. But that is not what hell is. Hell is simply you separating yourself from God. Hell is not something that God does to you. Hell is something that you do to yourself by not dealing with your blocks to God. Hell is my refusal to enter into a relationship with God. At the same time, heaven is being with God without anything coming between you and God. That's heaven. It happens as a result of accepting God's invitation, becoming open to a relationship by dealing with your blocks. So heaven and hell are things that we do to ourselves. God does not send you to hell. I doubt that it is a place. It is more of a spiritual state. There could be a place, but I think that it is more likely a state of our stubbornly protesting, "No way am I going to accept this concept of God. The hell with God. I don't care about that." Even when God reveals Herself to us, we just can't make the leap because we haven't started working on that yet. And you know what? People really do

Happiness That Is Guaranteed

go through hell on earth when they are not in relationship with God. Look at what is happening in the world. Look at how devoid the world is of being connected with God. The world is not devoid of God. The world is devoid of making connection with God. And this is why the world is in the state that it is in. This is the hell that we are in.

A second obstacle is the belief that if I do not see God, God does not exist. Too many of us give lip service to a belief in God when our daily actions do not reflect a belief in a God who cares about us at every moment. There are many things that we do not see that are real. If you've ever fallen in love, you cannot see the feeling of love itself. You cannot actually see love, but it is real; it's happening to you. How can it not be real? If you deny this, then you deny your own existence. Just as love is a very real experience, so is God. If you have experienced love, you have experienced God. Yet we constantly use our physical sight as a barrier to separate us from the true God. Somehow love is something other than God. Caring for another person is something other than God. But it is not. It is God. The belief that God has to be seen in order to exist is a myth, a fallacy. God does not have the limitation of having to be seen in order to exist. The need to be seen is part of the false gods. When we are depressed and want to feel good, we turn to gods we can see, such as sex, drugs, money, and even other people, for long-term fulfillment. But they never totally fill the void. They are false gods. However, there are many things such as love, which is the greatest of all the things that we do not see, yet it is very real.

A third obstacle that makes it difficult for people to recognize God within them is that they do not believe that God could dwell within them. They may not feel important, worthwhile, or confident or they may be afraid of the idea of God being with them. However, at any point in your life, if you have genuinely done something to help someone else, you have witnessed God within you. People who seem grumpy or moody every day have their moments when even they have offered a helping hand. Criminals, who are judged to be some of the worst people, have helped others at different points in their lives. No matter whether you are the worst person or the best person, when you reach out to another human being, God is manifested or made present through your showing love and concern for another.

Thus one way to overcome feeling uneasy about God dwelling within you is to become aware of your particular way of helping others. You may have saved someone's life or prevented an accident from occurring, or you may have done something as simple as helped someone with a chore such as grocery shopping or cleaning, which would have been more cumbersome if you had not offered your assistance. You may be thinking that anyone could have helped this person. This is true. But no one can help another person in the same way that you can. If you make someone feel better by listening and guiding them to the best solution to their problem, you did this in a way that no one could ever imitate exactly. Someone else also might have been successful in assisting this person in finding a solution to their problem, but they could never use your words in the same time sequence while conveying the impact of all your gestures and facial expressions to give the same assistance that you did. Just as no two people are alike, there are also no two people who will care for others in the same way; therefore, you are special because there will never be another you and because, in the history of the universe, whatever you do will never be repeated ever

Happiness That Is Guaranteed

again exactly as you did it. There are people in the world that you will have more of an impact on than anyone else because of the particular way you care and understand them. No one else can do this, only you. No one else has your uniqueness, personality, and characteristics that God has given you to draw people who are specifically attracted to your qualities. In order for you to draw or attract anyone, God must dwell in you. Ultimately, our happiness lies in being drawn to Love itself. One of the most powerful ways in which people are drawn to God is through another human being who has allowed love to dwell with him or her. If you do not celebrate your specialness manifested through your personality, then how difficult it is to celebrate God in you by being the vehicle through which others come to know Him.

FOOD FOR THOUGHT

Recall an occasion when a close friend wanted to spend time with just you. List why your friend would want to spend company with you and not with anyone else at this moment.

A fourth obstacle that separates us from God is that we are in the habit of associating God with images and entities that over time have acquired a negative reputation for us. Often we associate God with the image of a mother or a father; however, for those individuals whose relationship with their parents was strained or nonexistent, a parental image of God will not bring them closer to God. At other times, we associate God with a particular church or institution or with people in leadership; however, the problem with this is that no person or institution is perfect. When a person has a falling out with the church, their relationship with God tends to become less fervent and distant. Thus many people do not see a need to develop their relationship with God, because for years they had either consciously or unconsciously associated God with people, churches, institutions, or entities that can be mediums of God, but they are not God.

To develop a relationship with God, many of us need to change the images or objects we associate Her with. One way to do this is by associating Her with positive images that befits Her nature, who She is. When you think of God, instead of picturing a pervasively punitive father or mother, picture Her as a close friend who cannot wait to see you at the end of the day. He or she listens, understands, and sympathizes with you. You can spend hours in his or her presence. You know that your friend cares about you and is willing to do whatever he or she can to help you in time of need. This is the image that we are invited to associate with God. It corresponds to who She is as love; therefore, begin to associate Her with images of love and put yourself in the picture or scene. Consider the following: (1) Picture God as a person who gives you food when you are hungry. (2) She invites you into Her home when you have no place to stay. (3) She visits you in your time of illness. These examples are not farfetched, because you may have experienced some of them. If you have, realize that the person who helped you could not have done it if Love did not dwell in them.

The fifth obstacle is that for so many of us, God is stifling. We feel like there are all these rules and laws that we have to fulfill. And if we miss one, we are damned forever. God is constantly watching over our shoulders like a tyrannical supervisor waiting for one mistake to build a case for firing us. This is not God. This is not consistent

Happiness That Is Guaranteed

with love. God can also stifle us by not giving us any room to be creative. There is no room for error, no room for mistakes. I have to be perfect. But God does not demand that we be perfect; in fact, that is imperfect. To be perfect is to be imperfect: to make mistakes is to be perfect because in our mistakes, we learn and we grow. The perfect never grow. Do you know people who can do no wrong? Now really think about this. Are they growing? Do they strike you as really mature people, really creative people, people who are going to change the world? I hardly think so. Imperfect people who learn from their mistakes are the ones who do the most maturing. They are the ones who will change the world. So you are free of having to fit into the stifling mold of perfectionism. God does not want you in a mold. She wants you to be free in Her image, like Herself, not lacking anything, having no limits.

The sixth obstacle that prevents us from getting in touch with God is, how can God care about me after all of the bad things that have happened to me? You may have gone through the death of a loved one, the abuse of trust, the unfortunate mishaps that have caused more struggle and pain in your life, and not being able to find a suitable companion in your life. I keep getting these people who are abusive and don't seem to know how to communicate with me. How can God allow all these bad things to happen? It's a very tough question. It gets us to look at an age-old question of why do bad things happen to good people? We are not talking necessarily about things we have done. We can understand that if I gamble with my rent money or if I do not pay my bills on time, I can't blame God for that. But sometimes things happen that are out of our control. For instance, you are on your way to an emergency room where you make a living saving lives. You are walking across the street and are struck by a passing car. How could this have happened to someone who does so much good? For the most part, we live in a free world. Sure, some things are determined, like our birthday, our personality, our looks. Then there are other situations where we determine the outcome. The driver who hits us is also free. No one is holding a gun to his head, forcing him to whip around the corner at 40 mph. Yet why did God allow this? Again it comes down to freedom. God does not make us act in certain ways, whether they are good or bad. If She did, She would be going against Her nature, which is love. Therefore, one way of preventing bad things from happening is for us to be more responsible with our freedom. This is more of a reason for getting in touch with God. When we act from being influenced by the compassionate presence within us, our aggressive behavior is quelled. You have more concern for yourself and others. You say to yourself, "Oh, I do not want to whip around the corner at 40 mph, because there may be a child chasing a ball. If I need to be at an engagement, I will leave earlier." Responsible charitable behavior comes out of a sound relationship with God. God cannot take away your freedom nor anyone else's. In this sense, I guess we are our brother's keepers. What about the innocent victim? Why doesn't God interfere, stop the accident before it happens? To be perfectly honest, no one knows the answer to this question, except God. We could theorize all day that God saw some significant good coming out it and allowed the accident to happen based on these grounds. The victim is awarded $100,000, or he meets his spouse in the hospital. But what do you say to a mother who has lost her three-year-old son in the Oklahoma City bombing? What good could come out of this? In cases of senseless violence, we feel the fragility of human existence. We are mortal, and each day brings us closer to our impending death. Even if God saved us a thousand times (and She probably has), we are still going to die. While death is excruciatingly painful, it is the one thing that challenges us to stretch our minds the most. You see a loved one lying in a coffin, and somehow it's hard to believe that he or she is dead. In a sense, we are right. What you see before you is a dead body. But what you do not see is a spirit that is very much alive, freer than when it was encumbered by the materiality of the body. The spirit cannot die; it does not have a body that wears out. The spirit is the real presence of your loved one, who is conscious and happier than he or she has ever been. Now he or she can join with God directly, without having to maneuver around the confines of his or her body. Sure we miss our dear ones, but we must understand that our body is the last barrier between us and God. And deep down in my heart, I would not want to rob anyone of the bliss of being with God without anything coming between him or her and God. It is like two lovers who are imprisoned for a ten-year sentence in two different countries. They long to be with each other, yet they can only see each other for a five-minute interval that happens only once a year. How happy they will be ten years later when the prison doors open.

Sometimes what also separates us from getting in touch with God is the past. Some of us had experiences of being abandoned as a child, mistreated and abused physically, mentally, and sexually. Whatever the unfortunate conditions we had to withstand, sometimes we allow those conditions to be a reason to separate us from God. Why did God allow me to grow up in poverty? What kind of God would do that? Again, the world is free. There are things that happen in this world that we are not responsible for.

Some we are. But God cannot interfere with freedom. It's when we allow these terrible conditions to be a reason for separating us from God that things get worse. Everyone is going to have to suffer something in this life. No one is going to get through it unblemished. The first noble truth, as the Buddha put it, is that life is suffering. There is always something that we are going to have to endure. But it can be transcended. The issue isn't what happens to us; rather, it's how we perceive it. It's how we see the reality of God's connection with us. It's seeing the reality that we have all we need within ourselves to endure, to surpass, to move beyond any crisis. Instead of using that condition as an excuse to stay miserable and unhappy, we can use it as an opportunity to expand our vision to get a glimpse of the bigger picture that God sees.

An experience that I had on my sixteenth birthday may help us understand God's acting from a standpoint of having all knowledge. On the day of my sixteenth birthday, it seemed that everyone had forgotten. From morning to sunset, no one gave any indication that they remembered. When eight o'clock came, I had concluded that no one cared, and I could no longer hold back tears. I went to my room and pouted for about an hour until my mother called me to help her. When I emerged from my room, to my surprise, I was greeted by party streamers, presents, and many close friends and relatives' huddled around a sparkling birthday cake. As you can see, things did not happen the way I expected it. Like God, my close friends and relatives had information that I did not have. First, they were not going to let my birthday pass without celebrating it. Second, though I had given up all hope, eventually I received what I wanted, although it did not happen the way that I had planned for it. Often God operates in the same way. She does answer our prayers, respond to what we ask of Her if it is in accordance with Her nature of love. However, She does it in the best time and best way for us, which She knows through the schema of Her infinite wisdom. We think that our plan is the best plan, but if it does not coincide with God's plan, then it is not the best plan. It is not the best because we do not know how our plan will affect the rest of our lives, the people with whom we come in contact, and the other events that will happen in our lives. On the other hand, God's plan is the best plan, because having all knowledge, She knows how Her plan will affect, in the best possible way, our lives, other people, and events in our lives. Thus you will get what you want, but not always at the time or in the way you expect it. Therefore, do not stop talking with God because it seems that She neglects you. Instead, it is the opposite. She loves you so much and you are so special to Her that She does not want just any plan for you; She wants the best for you.

Another obstacle that inhibits our recognition of the divine within us is a tendency to separate God from the mainstream of our lives. We create a duality in our lives in which we assign God the role of predominantly taking care of everything that pertains to church and spirituality, and for anything else, She takes a back seat. Sometimes we feel that if we pursue a close relationship with God, then we cannot or should not become involved in other endeavors that can offer some healthy satisfaction. On the other hand, we feel that if we explore these endeavors, we cannot become too close to God. For example, when I was five years old, I felt my first desires to become a Catholic priest. Since then until well into my early adulthood, I received the message from certain significant people that if I were going to have a close relationship with God, I could not become too close to women. For a young man studying to be a Catholic priest, which I did for twelve years, women were viewed as temptations to sway you away from God and holiness. Romantic feelings were just another way in which our attention or focus would be taken off God; it seemed that if you are to draw close to God, what do you need romantic feelings for?

In the past few years, I have realized that romantic feelings and developing a close relationship with women or men do not have to inhibit a close relationship with God. In fact, they can enhance such a relationship by reminding us that the quality of our involvement with significant others hinges upon the depth of our commitment to God. I do not think that the people who advocated a separation of romance and God were totally unbalanced. I simply think that they did not put these experiences in proper perspective. There is nothing wrong with romance, because it can be a powerful means of experiencing God. We will elaborate more on this area when we cover the details of how to develop a closer relationship with God.

As you can see, separating God from our intimate relationships and the mainstream of our lives can cause us to wean Her out of the prominence that She deserves in our lives. There are many situations in our lives where we feel that we cannot become close to God while involved in certain activities. Right now, many of you are feeling that you cannot grow close to God for many reasons, perhaps because you like money, sex, drugs, or whatever your pleasure may be. However, your liking or disliking of these things does not have to be the deciding factor that keeps you from growing close to God and being happier than you have ever been in your life. But if you are feeling barred from closeness with Her because of whatever you are involved in or because of your desires, know that you do not have to be. One of the best ways to address this feeling so that you can begin to develop closeness is by honestly considering the following questions and ideas. Write down your answer to these questions. Often when we express ourselves by writing down our thoughts and feelings, we get a clearer picture of what is happening within us. And when we understand ourselves better, we can make better decisions concerning the course of our lives.

1. What are you involved in that inhibits you from developing your relationship with God?
2. Does it benefit you and others? If so, how?
3. Does it hurt or cause harm to you and/or others? If so, how?

These are critical questions, because if your endeavors are harming you or others, it is very difficult to have a relationship with God. Harming yourself or others is opposed to what God is all about, which is caring for yourself and others. If you have a friend who is always supportive of you, and you manipulate and use him or her for money, sex, or other objectives, then your friendship will not last. The same applies to God. There are people who cheat others through the mail, coworkers and supervisors who verbally and emotionally abuse each other, people who are inconsiderate and impolite or who constantly use foul language. These behaviors are opposed to a caring God, and they prevent many people from having the happiness they desire deep in their hearts. However, if in our honesty, we can admit to cheating, lying, or any other behavior that lacks care for ourselves and others on a small or large scale, we are on our way to changing these behaviors and obtaining lasting happiness.

On the other side, there are people who are involved in activities that benefit themselves and others. Yet they continue to feel awkward in their relationship with God, because their activities involve money, sales, romance, science, technology, or other areas that have the stigma of being in competition with God. Money, romance, science, etc., have become demigods that society parades before us as the objects of lasting happiness. Yet none of them can overcome the ultimate obstacle to happiness, the grave.

However, these prominent objects of society do not have to be in competition with God; instead, they can serve as a means of affirming Her by opening up opportunities that people can use to grow close to Her. For example, imagine that you are a car salesperson. You do not need to talk a fast game around a customer by using a gimmick or catch so that you can wheedle a few extra bucks out of him or her. Gimmicks are nothing more than deceptive traps. We wonder why we have so many deceptive people; it is built right into our system of goods and services that we use every day. Therefore, instead of using the deceptive approach, try being honest by informing the customer of the price of the product, tax and profit included. If the product is as good as you say it is, then it will practically sell itself. If you do not like this proposal, then devise one that will benefit both you and the customer without any deception, but with honesty.

This is not meant to be a lesson in sales, but it is a way to use money and sales as an opportunity to facilitate growth in one's relationship with God. This may sound awkward because we are not used to this concept, but it works. You may have seen it work. When a salesperson is

Happiness That Is Guaranteed

honest and fair with a customer, without using any gimmicks, a customer feels satisfied with a product or service. They know what they are getting. Generally, they feel that during the business transaction, the utmost care and concern were given to them.

For instance, yesterday I went to my car dealership to get my car battery's circuitry repaired. The service was excellent. I did not have to wait long. The customer service representative took the time to explain the problem and the type of repairs made. He was congenial, and he took interest in providing me service. He seemed honest and fair, and he did not appear to use any gimmicks. I felt that during the business transaction, the appropriate care and attention were given to me.

When you experience service like the kind rendered at my car dealership, you will usually return to that particular business. You will recommend it to your friends. Thus not only do you benefit from satisfying service but the business and sales personnel also benefit from a good reputation and returning customers. This is an approach to business, sales, and money that facilitates care and concern. When customers feel cared about and salespeople are supported by their customers, a congenial atmosphere prevails. Whenever people feel treated with care, honesty, and fairness, they generally feel good, important, and valued, which lays the foundation for them to treat others similarly. Through their concern for others, a foundation is being laid for their recognizing God within them as their love or care for others. People are more apt to want to find out more about God, the pervasive love in the world, and to allow Her to fill their lives. People are moving toward one another, instead of away from each other. When this happens, God is no longer placed in competition with money, sales, science, etc., because She is the power, care, and concern that brings people together. Money, business, and science are now a means through which people encounter God and are brought together. When people move toward each other, great things are accomplished.

This approach in which God is not in competition with money, business, and science, but is affirmed by them, is strongly needed in today's society. Because without it, the truth is that people are abused. As a result, they either abuse others or their self-esteem and hope for a better life are severely eroded.

Just the other day, a good friend told me that she felt that her employer and company were taking advantage of her. She works as the senior housekeeper in a hotel. Recently, her supervisor found new employment, thus leaving the supervisory position vacant. For two weeks, my friend not only worked her position as senior housekeeper, but she was given all of the supervisor's duties as well. However, although she had to take on the stress and workload of two jobs, her employer saved a few hundred dollars because he never paid her a cent of the money that would have gone to a supervisor, although she carried out the duties of that position. Unfortunately, this is happening all over the country. People are overstressed because they are working two or three jobs, but are only paid for one. This type of treatment of employees does not bring people together nor is it honest and fair. By the way, my friend wants to resign, but she won't because she needs the income; meanwhile, she must contend with the stress and her recently diagnosed thyroid condition. For the most part, business of this nature perpetuates the practice of keeping business at odds with Godlike qualities that not only make a business more successful, but can be a means of encountering God as a result of people coming together.

You begin to get in touch with the true God by becoming aware of the obstacles that separate you from God. The more aware you are of these obstacles and how they are preventing you from experiencing the fullness of your inner strength and power, the more the barriers between you and God will begin to crumble. A renowned author by the name of Anthony DeMello wrote a powerful book entitled *Awareness*. In his book, he makes the point that you and I can give someone all the advice in the world, but you won't change her. He emphasizes that the more aware an individual is of the reality of a difficult situation, she will begin to change herself. A crisis really doesn't change anyone. People experience crises every day and do not change. What changes someone is when she wakes up, becomes aware, and sees the unadulterated naked reality of the mess her life has become. Then, she changes. The same applies to getting in touch with God. We're never going to be happy and experience the fullness of fulfillment, feeling a sense of lacking nothing within ourselves, which only comes from developing a relationship with God, who lacks nothing. We are never going to have this if we are not aware of the watered-down version of life that most of us live. The watered-down version is pretending and believing that we can have the most fun, most excitement, most fulfillment without developing our relationship with God. You really haven't seen fun yet until you start to take little morning walks with God, when he will show you the universe as your amusement park. And during those walks, you will hear God's voice, your inner voice, tell you everything you need to know to accomplish your dreams and goals, which you thought were impossible. We are not talking about wearing God on your sleeve and imposing Her on other people; instead, we are talking about being in touch with the presence of God in the silence of your heart and allowing the power of Her presence to change your life forever. But it all starts with your awareness of the obstacles that now separate you from God. If you have read this chapter with openness, you have already begun to move closer to God.

Now you are ready to pursue your purpose in life, the positive life-giving endeavor or activity that you really love to do, that you can put into the service of humanity. When you start to do this, you are getting in touch with the true God of freedom. The obstacles that prevented you from seeing the true God are not as strong as they used to be. You are starting to develop an interest in God as the love that enables you to care more about yourself and others. A significant way to do this is by working on some endeavor that you enjoy doing and seeing how others can benefit from it. Why spend your life doing something you don't care much about? You will only be miserable in the long run, and you can't be of much service to others if you are miserable. However, when you care about yourself and others, you experience God. We sometimes speak of God as "Sophia," which is Wisdom. Wisdom is knowledge that comes out of freedom. God is freedom. When we hear God's reassuring voice and experience her caring for us despite our shortcomings, we feel so full within ourselves that we start to treat other people as God has treated us. We are free to care about others, no matter what their religion, color, culture, beliefs, opinions, or mishaps are. Our scope of vision, our judgment has been expanded so that we see beyond the petty judgments we used to burden people with. And now we see aspects of others that help us to respect their humanness. Besides, one thing that links all human beings is that we all have struggles and together we can help to lighten each other's burdens. When we see beyond other people's shortcomings and differences, our vision is unleashed and thus our judgment improves. We make decisions based on seeing the larger picture. Now we can choose a fulfilling purpose in life, because we have the vision to see how it will benefit not only ourselves but also the lives of other people.

Chapter 7

Pursuing Your Purpose in Life

What is your purpose in life? The answer to this question lies in finding your specific unique way of living out the love, energy, and passion within you, living out God within you. Your purpose is already within you, even if you are not aware of it yet. So how do you find your purpose in life? The first step is to ask yourself, what is it that would energize me and give me the most enjoyment? What is the activity or endeavor that I really love to do every day that is positive, life-giving, and benefits others? Take a moment and think about this question. Use the space provided to list the things that you could get the most enjoyment from doing every day and that could be put at the service of others.

1. _____ 6. _____
2. _____ 7. _____
3. _____ 8. _____
4. _____ 9. _____
5. _____ 10. _____

Once you make your list, start to prioritize these activities. Which activity would you enjoy the most? This may be difficult because there may be a variety of activities that you enjoy a great deal. Which one is most in line with who you are, your personality, the things that you are attracted to? If there were only one thing that you could do for the rest of your life, which one would you pick? You could possibly pursue two endeavors, but for now, let's stick to one because you don't want to overextend yourself early on. You don't want to be a jack of all trades, but a master of none. Also, do not worry that maybe you are making a mistake by choosing one activity over another, because whatever you are meant to do or whatever your real purpose in life is will emerge, sometimes even while you're working on another passion. The present activity that gives you enjoyment will lead you to the next step, which is something that may be more fulfilling. However, right now it may not be time for that. There is a time and a place for everything. But it is important that you start working on at least one thing that you are passionate about. Otherwise, you are delaying fulfillment in your life. And if you don't start, how can you be led to your real purpose if indeed what you are doing now is to be a stepping-stone to direct you to that path. Trust the energy, the compassion within you; it will not lead you astray.

The second step is to determine whether your purpose in life or dream is consistent with your inherent power, God. Does your purpose contradict love? Is it destructive of yourself and others? Dreams or goals that are not consistent with love will never bring you fulfillment. A sinister goal may be accomplished, but it always falls short of providing lasting fulfillment. It doesn't have sustaining power, which is fueled by compassion. Hitler had a dream of advancing the Aryan nation by any means necessary, which included the genocide of the Jews. But although Hitler made significant strides in achieving his ends, he failed miserably. His goal was not aligned with love, the infinite power that guarantees victory. Thus your dreams need to be consistent with love; otherwise, you set out to accomplish something that will not bring you fulfillment in the first place. Therefore, you need to ask yourself: Is my goal or passion destructive of myself and others? Does it enhance my life and the lives of others? If not, then I need to readjust my goal or take up another dream or passion that befits love. For instance, if my dream is to become a rap artist and my lyrics glamorize drugs and debase women, I could bring more fulfillment into my life by aligning my dream with my inherent power of love. This could take the form of discouraging drug use and lifting up women.

Another example is of a friend whose goal is to reduce drug use through substance abuse treatment. At one point, he resolved to live his life smoking marijuana and attending as many parties as he could. However, after getting into one bad relationship after another and after losing control of how much marijuana he was using, he decided to implement a recovery program in his life. As a result, not only has he maintained abstinence for ten years but he has also taken steps to begin a private practice to treat substance abuse. By changing his dream or passion to be more consistent with his inner power, he has enabled more satisfaction and peace to enter his life.

Once you have identified your dream that enhances you and others, the third step is to take small steps toward accomplishing your goal. This step should be some action that you can see yourself doing. It doesn't require much effort. Make it something that is fun or interesting. It could be as simple as making a telephone call to register for a class or to gather information about how you could become involved in your field of interest. It could also take the form of developing a tentative plan. However, at this stage, it is best not to overwhelm yourself with cumbersome tasks; instead, take small light tasks to put you on the road to working on your dream. If you start with difficult tasks, you are increasing the likelihood of abandoning your dream because you burn yourself out early, instead of building yourself up slowly to take on the more difficult aspects. This is an efficient way to use energy, and it exercises your endurance muscles so that your dream can reach fruition. When you build muscles to strengthen your body, you do not start by lifting weight that will immediately overwhelm the muscle. You start gradually with light weight. The same applies to building endurance muscles for accomplishing your dream. Start with small tasks and work your way up to the more difficult ones. By doing this, you are getting yourself used to what it takes so that when strenuous challenges emerge, you will have the stamina to weather them and attain your goal.

When we start to take the small steps, it's common to loose motivation and enthusiasm. We may procrastinate, lose interest, and eventually abandon our dream. This may happen because we have found a new endeavor that motivates us more. However, when we start to pursue our new purpose, we will most likely run into the same problem, and we may eventually find ourselves putting it aside. At times like these, when you want to accomplish your dream, but find yourself working on everything except your dream, you are being confronted most likely with your own fear. We stop tenaciously pursuing our dream because we are afraid that we won't succeed. Therefore, we procrastinate, don't take risks, become lazy, and make excuses that mask our underlying fears. Consequently, we remain in what is called our comfort zone. This is where we stick to things that we are used to, things that do not cause any waves. We know what to expect. Our comfort zone takes the form of a typical day during the work week. For the most part, we know what is going to happen. We follow our regular routine of getting up at the sound of the alarm, showering, going to a job where you know what to expect, coming home to dinner, watching television, sleep, and the whole thing starts all over again the next day. Our comfort zone can also take the form of performing only those tasks that we are absolutely convinced that we can do. Two weeks ago, I cleaned my entire home in four consecutive days. During that time, I was invited to gatherings, but I declined the offers because I was determined to finish my cleaning. It was amazing that I did not let anything distract me. However, I wondered why I was so diligent in my cleaning, yet when it came to other goals, such as my writing, I could easily put them aside. After analyzing my behavior, I realized that the reason I could be so committed to cleaning my home, yet procrastinate in my writing, was because I was confident that I could do a good job cleaning. I knew that by thoroughly cleaning with soap, water, and furniture polish, I would end up with a beautiful apartment every time. It was easy, predictable, and consistent with my comfort zone. However, with my writing, I am not convinced that I can eventually arrive at a good product. I worry too much about whether I am doing it right and using the right words. Underneath my procrastination and excessive criticism is my fear that I won't come out with a good book. Therefore, I forgo opportunities to write, become easily distracted, and am at a high risk for abandoning my dream. Often we are at risk for giving up our dream if we have a fear of not succeeding.

The first thing that you need to do to overcome fear is to recognize it. Admit that you are afraid of not succeeding. Become aware of the impact of the consequences of forgoing your dream. Also, become aware of the many ways your life will be enhanced if you accomplish your dream despite your fear. The second step may surprise you.

Happiness That Is Guaranteed

It is to realize that there is no such thing as failure; it's an illusion. There is no way that you are not going to succeed. The only time failure exists is when you refuse to learn another way of getting around an obstacle. There are many people who go 90 percent of the way to achieving their goal and then they stop. They figure that there isn't another alternative, perhaps something else they were missing before, that they can learn and employ to take them the rest of the way. Successful people will tell you that they endured many challenges and dark nights, but they never ceased learning and applying what they learned to surpass the obstacles to their success. Therefore, you cannot fail. The only way that you will not succeed is if you refuse to learn and employ an alternative way of overcoming the challenges that stand between you and your dream.

Knowing that you cannot fail helps to motivate you to take the small steps toward your goal. In the process, it is important to coordinate these small steps into a plan.

A plan is like a road map. It directs and guides you to take certain roads to reach your destination. Although, it doesn't always warn you of detours, it points you in the right direction. Our plan for attaining our goals works similarly. Although it doesn't forewarn us of all of our challenges, it gives us direction. Without a plan that tells us which steps to take and when to implement them, we simply have a bunch of great ideas, but no means of making them happen.

Therefore, first it is extremely helpful to get a daily planner, which is a notebook that lists the days of the week and in which you can write specific goals or tasks for each day and how long they should take. In this way, if your goal or a segment of your dream will take a few months to accomplish, you have a viable tool to measure your progress. Following an organized schedule also helps reduce procrastination and gives you a clear picture of where you want to go and how to get there.

When you schedule in the specific steps for accomplishing your goal, first make sure that they are steps that you can see yourself doing; they are doable. If it is something that you need to do, but you find it a bit overwhelming, break the task down into smaller steps that you can see yourself doing.

Second, make sure that these steps are not vague or too general. Be specific. Vaguely stated or broad tasks are a major reason why they are not doable. It's difficult to complete a task when you are not sure what the task is. Instead of scheduling a task such as "from 1:00 p.m. to 3:00 p.m., find information about the art of writing." You can make this more specific and clear by scheduling "from 1:00 p.m. to 3:00 p.m., go to the library and take notes on the critically acclaimed book, *The Art of Writing*, by John Trumble." With specific action steps, you save more time and you are more focused on your goal; thus you attain your goal or dream sooner.

Sometimes your schedule may not always go according to plan. It may take you longer to complete a task than anticipated. This is all right. Simply adjust your schedule to accommodate your need for more time. But please, do not become lax in using a daily planner, because things never seem to go according to plan. Always plan how to accomplish your goal. When you don't plan, you cannot anticipate mistakes that could be avoided; therefore, you waste a lot of time, and you create more confusion for yourself than you would have otherwise. Ultimately, without a plan, the odds of abandoning your dream are

Happiness That Is Guaranteed

greater because you would lack concrete direction and you wouldn't have the ongoing focus that a plan provides.

Besides planning, you must be willing to make sacrifices. You must be willing to do without some things so that you can bring joy into your life by doing what you love. But rather than looking at this as giving up something, we become more productive if we look at sacrifice as the things we give toward our dreams. By doing without one thing, I open up a space to put time, energy, and whatever else it takes into doing what I love. Therefore, sacrifice is what you are willing to *give* in order to bring more joy into your life. For example, when I was a child, my mother was willing to give her time, which she would have otherwise spent on recreation and relaxation, to work three jobs. She made this sacrifice so that her dream of raising three healthy sons could be realized. Right now, there are people who are turning their lives around and committing themselves to their own happiness. They are giving time and energy to do what they love. They are working a part-time job and living on much less than what they are used to so that they can work on their dream. Because they are living on much less, they don't rent movies from video stores. They don't eat out, make long distance calls, and take exotic vacations. They pay for and use only those things that are absolutely necessary, like their rent or mortgage, utilities, and food. They conserve water, electricity, and other energy sources. Their act of doing without, sacrificing even for a short time, is their gift toward their dream. It is not easy to do without things that you are used to. But it is worth it when you consider that the gift of your sacrifices is an important means leading to the attainment of your dreams.

Gregory F. Bearstop

In pursuing your goal or purpose in life, it is most important that you not become too focused on achieving the goal. It does not matter whether you achieve the goal or not. What matters is whether you enjoyed the process. For example, when you are running a race and you are too focused on winning a gold medal, you become nervous and tense; you lock up. You are not able to stretch out with large limber strides needed to win. Recall the Olympic Games of 1996 in Atlanta, Georgia. Most of the winners of gold medals were asked how they were able to win the gold medal. They all responded similarly by saying that they were not focused so much on the gold medal but that they wanted to enjoy the opportunity to do their best. This attitude put them in a relaxed confident state that enabled them to attain their goal. The same is true for you. If you enjoy the process, you will have peace of mind that will enable you to make the best decisions and to take the appropriate actions that will make your dreams come true.

While accomplishing any dream, you are bound to run into situations that will cause you to risk giving up your dream. Expect it. For instance, suppose that you feel that your purpose in life is to open a business. You need to take out a loan, but all you receive is rejection every time. There doesn't seem to be any way to obtain the money to open your business. Though this is the one thing that you have always wanted to do, the easiest way out is to give up. Over time we become weary of enduring the hardships, the rejections, and the lack of support. We resolve to go back to living the same old dull life that we had before.

You may be in the middle of working on your dream and are devastated because a loved one has died. You may have been stricken by a serious illness. You may be so deep in debt that you don't know what to do. On the other hand, all three of these situations may be happening to you all at once. At times like these, you will say, "I can't handle this. I can't take this. This is too much." What you are doing is crying out for something more, something stronger and greater than you, because you know that you cannot overcome these challenges by yourself. What will happen is, when the challenges become overwhelming, we give up. We have to if we are still stuck in the mind-set that I have to overcome these things by myself. You are not supposed to handle them by yourself in the first place. The emotional strain is too much. These challenges remind us that by ourselves we are not enough. For those who choose to carry the weight alone, some of them commit suicide. The others die of a slow suicide through depression, violence, drugs, and so on. There is only so much a human being can take. But often what we don't realize is that within us, we have something stronger and greater than us. We have the power of the human spirit, the power of God within us. No goal, no dream, no purpose in life will ever be accomplished to its fullness without plugging into and developing a relationship with the power within you, developing a relationship with God. Sure, you may accomplish your dream, but it is always going to fall short of providing lasting fulfillment if you are not in touch with the power within you to overcome any obstacle in your path. This may seem strange. We don't often think that we need God to accomplish our dreams. Yet, that is where we experience our happiness, peace of mind, the feeling that everything is going to be all right.

I have a friend whose dream is to have a successful business making and selling hot sauce. Currently, he works a full-time job at a dry cleaner's; however, his biggest obstacle that prevents him from attaining his dream is his alcoholism. He drinks to cope with life. He loves everything about drinking: the taste, the smell, how it helps him to forget his problems and concerns and puts him at ease. Yet as a result, the past two years have been a nightmare. About a year ago, his wife and kids left him. He had conflicts with his employer and coworkers on the job. His van was in the repair shop every week. And he was in bad health.

However, four months ago, he went through an awakening. He told me that if he kept drinking, something horrible was going to happen to him. He also realized that he was always making excuses for not going to Alcoholics Anonymous meetings, where he could receive support and guidance in his recovery. Eventually, when he started to attend the meetings, he met people who gave him a ride to work when his van was broken. He had people with whom he could talk through his cravings for alcohol. As a result, his life has been 100 percent better. Since he has been going to support meetings and associating with people in recovery, he has started to rely on God. At times when he gets the temptation to drink, he hears God's voice within him saying, "You don't need alcohol. I am with you. You are doing so well. I love you." For the first time in his life, he really feels loved without strings attached. The more he listens to the voice of God, the compassionate presence within him, he says that his life has been better than anything he could ask for. He has a wonderful woman in his life who has a candlelight dinner prepared for him when he comes home from work. Moreover, his employer is giving him a free company van.

He recently discovered that he has prostate cancer. This has caused much anxiety in his life. Because he is in touch with the presence of love within him, he says that he is not worried. He knows that if he continues to listen to the voice of God, things are going to work out. He has this faith. Also, his business of selling hot sauce is starting to get off the ground. Now he doesn't need alcohol, which has prevented him from working on his dream. Instead, he is in touch with the source of life within him that no one can take away. He is in touch with God, who constantly reaffirms him and is always by his side. God is his pillar of strength to overcome his most difficult challenges.

You can accomplish your dream not only by employing the right strategies and techniques, but also by developing your relationship with God. There are many people writing about how to fulfill your dreams. They emphasize the technical aspect, the strategic aspect, but very few emphasize that you need to be in touch with God in order to accomplish your dream and at the same time experience the fullness of fulfillment. There are many people who accomplish their dreams and then afterwards are depressed. They reach the summit. Now what? Is this it? Is this all there is? Unfortunately, they spend the rest of their lives depressed or suicidal. But real fulfillment comes from being in touch with the wellspring of freedom, feeling free every day. We feel unending love every day. And that comes from listening to the reassuring voice of God within us. We cannot attain our goals in life without endurance and perseverance. You can have all the technical skills in the world, but what the experts don't tell you is that endurance comes only from God. Whether you are aware of God's presence or not, that is where it comes from. You don't have to be aware. But if you are in touch with your spirit, then you will have endurance and perseverance. We see it in the Olympic games. People come through incredible odds to win gold medals. You can bet that every step of the way, they are listening to the reassuring voice that tells them, "You can. It's in your reach." Therefore, while pursuing your dream, you may get fulfillment from doing what you love, but you are falling short if you don't develop your relationship with God.

CHAPTER 8

DEVELOPING YOUR RELATIONSHIP WITH GOD

THE FIRST STEP

How do I make contact with God? In chapters 5 and 6, we actually began to take the first step in getting in touch with God, which is **to be introduced to Him**. We began to see God as the power within us, and we became more aware of the obstacles that separate us from Him. There are many ways to meet God. We can be introduced to God when someone tells us about who He is. We can meet Him through revelation of His Word, through Holy Scripture. We can also have an experience in which we feel or encounter His presence. Some people report feeling a warm sensation that is unlike any feeling that they have ever had. These experiences can take place anywhere. However, although they may spark our interest for a while, they may not initially motivate us to pursue a relationship with God. This is not unusual. It can be a part of the developmental stages of any relationship. Many of us have friends whom we were not fond of in the beginning, but over time, we seem to gravitate toward one another. The same is true with God. Weeks, months, years may go by before we reach a point where we desire to pursue a relationship with God. But, instead of taking months or years, it is possible to begin to develop a relationship with God right now and to obtain from this day onward, more happiness than you've ever had.

THE SECOND STEP

The second step to develop your relationship with God is **to recognize a significant quality that God has which is also present in you**. If you can pick out this quality and cultivate it to the point where it draws you to God, then your relationship with Him can mature, which will lead to unspeakable joy.

There are several qualities that God has to an infinite degree that we also have to a lesser degree. In fact, God is the love, care, and concern within us. When we do not recognize God or the Divine within us as being our love, care and concern for others, we rob ourselves of the unspeakable joy that only love can give. Maybe one major reason why some people become easily annoyed, hardened, or even criminals in the first place is because they stop recognizing God within them.

When you develop a relationship with someone, you are initially attracted to him or her because you recognize something about that person that is also in you. For instance, you might like a friend who has a pleasant and peaceful disposition. On the other hand, when you look within yourself, you will find that you are generally a peaceful person or have a great desire for peace. Therefore, one reason that you are drawn to your friend is because either both of you possess a similar quality or you see a quality in the other that you want to cultivate in yourself to give you more of a feeling of wholeness.

The way in which we begin to develop a relationship with our friends is similar to how we come to meet God. We become fond of or attracted, in the sense of being drawn, to God initially because we see qualities in God that we desire to cultivate in ourselves. Therefore, we are motivated to find out more about Him by getting to know who He is, which we can never know entirely, and by spending time with Him.

The most significant quality is the ability to love or show care and concern for ourselves and others. Love is most significant because all other virtues and qualities hinge upon it. Without love or some degree of care and concern, there would be no peace, justice, hope, or any other right-minded principle. Since it is the heart of all the other virtues, it is the most Godlike quality we possess. Therefore, what we need in order to become interested in God and drawn to Him is first to recognize the ability to love that is in each of us. If we refuse to acknowledge our ability to love, then we become hardened individuals and we close the door to a life of fulfillment and peace. This is why on the news we hear about and see pictures of murderers, and people who commit crimes not including white-collar crimes, because maybe this is their way of getting some satisfaction by channeling their pain upon society. Yet I have never heard of a hardened individual who struck me as being truly happy. Thus the second step for developing a relationship with God is recognizing our ability to love or to show care and concern for others, self, and God. This act contains the seeds for stimulating our interest in God and drawing us closer to Him.

Therefore, the care and concern that we show to others or the love within us is God in us. When we recognize love in us, we recognize God in us. This is why, unlike the qualities, characteristics, and traits that we may have in common with our friends, the ability to demonstrate love is amazingly unique.

When you genuinely show concern by helping someone or even helping yourself, you experience warmth that feels good and fulfilling. It is similar to the feeling of falling in love, when you are so caught up in pleasure with the other that everything around you looks so beautiful. Even though you may not feel love to this extent, it is still a pleasurable feeling just the same. When you experience the pleasure that you will get from loving and helping yourself or others, you will want to feel this more often; therefore, you will want to do more caring actions to maintain the satisfaction that you are receiving. In the process, either consciously or unconsciously, you are becoming more fond of God, who is the love, care, and concern that you show to others and yourself.

A good example of the attraction of love through caring is an incident that occurred a few months ago when twelve children witnessed an elderly woman being robbed. All of those kids rushed over to the lady to defend her from the assailant. As a result, the kids were able to entrap the robber and rescue the lady from further harm. All of the children were honored with awards for their heroic deed.

In essence, these kids showed love to the defenseless lady by rescuing her from the robber. They felt much pleasure and satisfaction because of their good deed. In addition, they felt even more satisfaction because they received recognition for their efforts. We could venture that the next time these kids feel that they can help someone in need, they probably will. Their benevolent actions will be reenforced by the good feeling of getting a personal sense of satisfaction from making another person's life a little better, as well as their own. Therefore, when they or any of us do something that helps ourselves and others in a healthy life-giving way, we take an initial step in establishing a relationship with God. We are like the person who strikes up an interest in a potential friend because he recognizes a quality in him or her that would make him feel complete.

It is not enough to just show love for others if our aim is to grow closer to God. There are a lot of people who do nice things for others, yet they do not acknowledge God in their lives. God is with them, but they do not know it. Remember that there are also loving people who are atheists. However, if you want lasting happiness, you must draw close to God. If you want to accept God's invitation to develop a close relationship with Him, you need to recognize Him within you and in your care for yourself and others.

THE THIRD STEP

The third step in developing your relationship with God is **to communicate with God**. It is having communion with Him, being focused on Him. More specifically, it is becoming aware of God's presence and responding to that presence. God is always present with us, and every person on this earth from the day of your birth has always responded to God. You and I are constantly communicating with God even when we are unaware of it. To get a better understanding of this, it is helpful to look at what communication is.

First, communication is expressing yourself. We express ourselves in numerous ways such as through dancing, making sounds, gestures, movement of various parts of our body, actions, our works, and even through our very existence; our existence and the existence of everything else living and nonliving say something. As long as we are present on this earth, we are always expressing something in various ways. Since God is always with us, we are always communicating some message to God, whether verbally or non-verbally. Even when we are not saying anything to Him, we are communicating or giving off vibes, a certain mood such as satisfaction, depression, anger, peace, or love. These moods may not be directed to God; nonetheless, He knows what you are feeling. Sometimes we experience this with our friends. Has anyone ever told you that he or she was feeling fine, but your intuition told you that something was wrong with him or her? Then later you find out that your intuition was right. Similarly, through our body language, demeanor, and mood, we communicate to others and to God our feelings, thoughts, and beliefs, even without saying a single word.

If we go days, weeks, or years without saying anything to God or acknowledging His presence, we communicate to Him the message that He is not our priority. He is the one who sustains our life, yet we have no time for Him. We only call on Him when we need something or when we are in church. This is often the limit of our response to Him. If you went months or years without talking to a close friend, imagine how hurt he or she would be and how much he or she would miss you.

Therefore, no matter what we do or say, we are communicating some kind of message to God. If we always try to care for ourselves and others in a way that is life giving, we send the message to God and others that we are oriented to do the loving and right thing. But if, for instance, we abuse drugs, lie, cheat, or steal from others to support our drug habit, we send the message that we do not care a lot about ourselves and others; all that we seem to care about is getting high. On the other hand, if we do acknowledge His presence by telling Him our thoughts and feelings and listening to His response, we communicate our desire to have a relationship with Him. When this happens, our lives take on new meaning, and we begin to feel the joy of lacking nothing.

While we are expressing ourselves to God, He is constantly expressing Himself to us. First, He does this through creation. Everything created tells us something about God. One of the most powerful messages that He expresses through all of creation is the invitation to be with Him. When you see a beautiful sunset, you are caught up in the moment. You are drawn to the beauty of this scene. As you experience this, you are being called to open yourself more to receive the invitation to be with God because He is the one who draws you to the sunset in the first place. He brings all things together in harmony.

God also expresses Himself through people who treat us as He would. One example of this is through the experience of falling in love. When two people come together in love, their concern for each other is so great that it leads them to commit themselves to each other forever. Through a couple's committed love, God communicates His unfathomable love to each of them because He is the love itself that sustains their commitment.

Thus God is always communicating with us through the things and people whom He created, and we are constantly communicating with Him by the way we live in the world. Either we communicate a lack of interest in Him by not recognizing His presence or we show our devotion to Him by daily acknowledging His presence and responding affirmatively to His invitation to be with Him. Therefore, the issue is not *whether* we communicate with God; rather, it is *what* we communicate. And this depends upon *how* we communicate. For example, if we speak to God in a way that indicates that we want to hurry up and get this over with, then we are telling Him that we have more important things to do. Just imagine if someone spoke to you in this manner; you would probably want to get up and leave. Similarly, how we communicate has everything to do with what we communicate. Therefore, in taking the third step, we will first focus on how to communicate with God in a way that can bring you closer to Him.

TIME

Many people become too focused on the idea of needing a lot of time to develop one's relationship with God. Instead of emphasizing the amount of time, it is more important to focus on whether you spend any time at all with God. Beginning with five or ten minutes a day is better than no time at all. As you experience the satisfaction and the fulfillment that those five or ten minutes will bring, you will automatically find yourself spending more time with God. However, for now, concentrate on setting aside five minutes a day to spend in God's presence. You will benefit most from this experience if you pick a time during the day when you are alert; it does not matter if you choose the morning, afternoon, or evening, as long as you take some time out for you and God. Even make an appointment for you and God in your daily schedule and don't let anything, other than an emergency, prevent you from keeping this appointment. If a friend wants you to do something at 2:00 p.m. and this is your time with God, kindly explain, "I'm sorry, but I have an appointment at this time. Let's meet in 20 minutes or at another time." If you regard your time with God as sacred, you will not believe how peaceful and joyful your life will become.

Happiness That Is Guaranteed

For people who do not seem to have a free moment, there is one option you can try. While you are doing chores such as the laundry, washing dishes, or any other chore, you can use the occasion to become aware of God's presence and speak to Him. If we can sing and talk on the telephone while we do chores, we can also talk to God. However, setting aside a specific time to speak with God is ideal. Remember, when you spend time with God, you are spending time with a close friend. Just as we must talk with our close friends, we must talk with God. He awaits you with the enthusiasm of a person who is about to reunite with his or her best friend, whom he or she has not seen in years.

Location

While the place and atmosphere can enhance your prayer time, you do not have to be in a particular place in order to pray; you can pray anywhere. However, if you have the luxury of a quiet, tranquil atmosphere, take advantage of it. You can use a peaceful haven in your home, perhaps a favorite room, that helps you to become aware of God's presence; it is certainly convenient if you have a busy schedule. However, you do not have to limit your place to any particular location; at times, a park, nature trail, the banks of a river or stream, or a small chapel may be a conducive place for encountering God. Everyone has different preferences. You will benefit more from prayer if you go to a place that appeals most to you.

Mood and Atmosphere

Often a certain mood or atmosphere can be a powerful means of experiencing God. The type of atmosphere that you might want to capture is one that gives you a feeling of transcendence or of being uplifted. This mood or feeling can be achieved through the use of certain objects or symbols that stimulate and appeal to your spirit. For instance, the use of candles can evoke a solemn feeling that helps you to become attuned to the reality of a significant presence. The billowy smoke of incense captures a sense that we are surrounded by a presence that is profound and mysterious. The sweet aroma of incense elicits a desire to draw close to and unite with God. Pictures, statues, and other representations and images are all means to help you focus and remember certain things about God that can enhance your experience of Him.

At this point, I invite you to pick a time that you can spend five or ten minutes in the presence of God. Make sure it is a time of the day when you are relatively alert. You will benefit more from this experience if you pick a time during the day when you are a little calmer and are alert. I also invite you to select a place that enables you to become aware of the divine presence. Once you have done this, you are now ready to develop a relationship with God that can make your life more joyous and happier than it has ever been.

Another element where God is present that can also give us a powerful experience of Him is His word, a written account of His revealing Himself to humankind. You can select a scriptural passage to which you feel drawn, or pick one that seems to apply to a situation that you are wrestling with. After you have read the passage over a few times and have absorbed its meaning, you can meditate upon or think about the implications that it has for your life. The wisdom and insight you gain from meditating upon the passage can be taken to God during the time you spend with Him.

The use of music that soothes and uplifts the spirit can assist in putting you in touch with God. As you can see, there are a variety of symbols that can be helpful in setting the tone for entering into the presence of God. At the same time feel free to be creative; use symbols that have a personal significance for connecting you with God. You can use any combination of symbols, or do not use any at all. The aim here is to employ symbols and practices that are life-giving and that open you to encountering God.

POSTURE

A fourth preparation that we want to consider as we enter God's presence is our posture, the position and demeanor of our bodies. As we have often seen, someone's posture can tell you much about how open he is to you and to what you are expressing. For instance, have you ever experienced losing someone's attention for a moment while you were talking with him? He began staring into space, or he started struggling to keep his eyes open. Finally, when you regained his attention, you had to repeat something that you said earlier. Although his body was physically present with you, his body language or posture told you that he was not listening. Oddly enough, we can do the same thing to God. For instance, have you ever noticed someone crossing his arms or legs while you were talking with him? This gesture or posture might have felt comfortable, but to the listener, it is still a barrier to communication. If you were speaking with someone who had his or her arms crossed as opposed to someone whose arms were relaxed, who would you feel was more open to what you had to say? Crossed legs and especially crossed arms sends an emphatic message that I am not totally open to this dialogue or to you. I do not want you to get too close. Unfortunately, you can use these and similar gestures and postures to keep God at a distance. Just as your posture can affect your openness with others, it can also affect how open you are with God. Therefore, you will benefit immensely if, in prayer, you assume postures that show a willingness to be open to God. Postures that facilitate openness are positions of the body such as the following: (1) Sitting with your back fully supported, arms and hands resting in your lap, and your feet flat on the floor; (2) standing without slouching; and (3) lying on one's back without crossing one's legs. There are also variations of these positions. For instance, instead of lying on your back, you could lie on your side. Instead of sitting with your hands in your lap, you might want to outstretch your arms. Feel free to experiment with other positions that send a message of openness that may feel more comfortable.

EXERCISE

Now you are in a place of relative peace for a few minutes. You have employed a few symbols, although they are not necessary to assist in uplifting your spirit. You have assumed a posture of openness. I now invite you to close your eyes. At this point, something very exciting is about to happen. You are about to enter a holy and sacred realm. Therefore, relax and be calm because you do not have anything to worry about anymore. To help you relax, I invite you to picture the top of your head. Once you can see the top of your head, quietly tell it to relax. Move down to your forehead and brain; tell them to relax. Let the muscles in your head go; let them loosen up and become limber. Sense how good it feels to loosen those muscles. Continue to move downward and relax your eyes, nose, mouth, ears, and cheeks. Tell your neck to relax. Let your shoulders go. Let your arms and hands go. Tell your chest and stomach to relax. Feel the muscles in your chest and stomach relax. Let the muscles in your buttocks go. Tell your legs, ankles, and feet to relax. Feel the muscles in your legs, ankles, and feet loosen. Tell your whole body to relax. Picture relaxation as warm soothing water being poured all over you. Now that you are relaxed, you are ready to enter a holy and sacred place, the realm of experiencing God's presence. To do this, I invite you to maintain the calm and relaxation that you have received as you begin to become aware of God's presence. At this time, I invite you to turn your thoughts in the direction of those experiences that manifest the love of God, because wherever love is, God is present.

Recall an experience when you strongly felt love. It was either an experience in which you showed care and concern for yourself or for others or an experience in which much care or concern was shown for you. In either instance, you felt the warmth and sensation of love. At this point, it may be helpful to close your eyes in order to visualize the experience. Relive it. Notice the surroundings. What was the weather like? What time of day was it? Describe in detail the room or place where the experience occurred. See the people involved. To the best of your knowledge, describe what they wore. Put yourself back into the experience, and relive it now just the way it happened. Say and do everything you did when you strongly felt love. Envision everyone else saying and doing everything exactly the way he or she did it.

As you relive your experience of love, you will begin to feel love within you. The love itself that you are feeling is God. As you feel care and concern for God, yourself, or others, you are experiencing God. Become aware of God as the love, care, and concern that you feel. Stay with this feeling. Enjoy it. Savor it. The concern that you receive from others or give to others is, at the same time, one way God shows His love for you. Right now, He is present in the affectionate feelings that you have.

Become aware of the many ways that God is loving you right now. He loves you by (1) being a God who is love; without Him, there would be no love, peace, justice, forgiveness, hope, or any other virtue; (2) always being with you; now we are aware of Him; and (3) sustaining your life because the next minute your life could end; we are not guaranteed tomorrow. Take a moment and recognize some of the ways that God loves you.

At any point during your recognition of His love, feel free to tell Him how you feel about the way that He loves you. You can also express your thankfulness and gratitude for His gifts. After you have expressed your feelings, it is imperative that you remain silent for a few moments and listen. Often we do not hear God speaking because we do most of the talking. We interpret silence as a void that needs to be filled with more talking and petitioning or as a signal that our prayer time is coming to an end. Contrary to this interpretation, silence is the opportunity to listen to God's voice; thus silence is the treasure of prayer.

RECOGNIZING THE VOICE OF GOD

How can you recognize the voice of God? After you have expressed your thoughts and feelings to God, you must remain silent in order to hear God's voice. In the silence, it may be difficult to hear His voice, your inner voice, because there are many voices which represent

Happiness That Is Guaranteed

aspects of our personality that are constantly jockeying for dominance in our mind. These voices can be narrowed down to three distinct voices: (1) your voice or words, (2) the voices of others, and (3) God's voice. How do you distinguish these voices? This is not an easy task. Many people have written extensively on this subject, and they offer several methods; however, I will share with you a powerful strategy that I use for recognizing God's voice.

First, we need to identify the different voices. Usually your voice is the one that is constantly reasoning, analyzing, and talking. Your voice gives you an underlying feeling that you are searching for some answer, for a solution, and for self-assurance. It tries to validate your thoughts and feelings. However, after you have weighed all the angles to a problem or concern, identified all the consequences, and have not reached a solution, then cease trying to figure things out. The way to silence your voice is to stop thinking so much; instead, tell yourself to calm down and relax. You don't have to say anything or do anything. Just let yourself be. If the chatter and reasoning start again, then patiently refocus on calming yourself. This will help to quiet your voice.

While quieting your voice, you may have heard the voices of others. They simply told you what you ought to do or should do. They may be right, or they may be wrong, but, for the most part, if you are hearing what you should do, you are hearing the voices of others. The way to silence their voices is to thank them and tell them that you are looking for God's voice. God will never tell you what you *should* do. He will also not beat around the bush; instead, He will be more forthcoming in whatever He desires to communicate.

Gregory F. Bearstop

When your voice and the voices of others have quieted, you will begin to hear the voice of God. His voice will excite you and give you enthusiasm. You will know His voice by recognizing these basic characteristics:

1. The voice of God is the voice of the compassionate presence in you. It affirms you and builds your self-esteem. It always has your best interests in mind. It looks out for your well-being and everyone else's.
2. The voice of God will not put you above everyone else, nor put everyone else above you. This voice will not come in the form of grandiose illusions. If the voice says that it is calling you to be a great prophet, you can bet that it is also calling others to be great prophetic voices in the world.
3. The voice of God corresponds to Holy Scripture. He will not direct you to do anything that contradicts the revelation of His Holy Word. He is not going to tell you to persecute someone because you don't like his or her attitude.
4. God's voice is persistent. He will not cease communicating a message until you receive and understand it. At times, His voice will hound you; it will not let you rest until you heed it. However, His voice does not hound you in the sense of annoying you; instead, it is a call to focus on things that matter most, and, in your gut, you know that it is a call to something wonderful.
5. God's voice is confident. For example, in regard to this book, I heard the words, "Get up and write." God was not telling me that He thinks that it might be a good idea to write; instead, He came across as

knowing exactly what He wanted to say, without a shadow of a doubt.
6. It challenges us to grow, not in the sense of putting us down, but in the sense of challenging our narrow beliefs that actually limit the amount of joy that we could have in our lives.

With the rise of religious fanaticism depicted in events like the Jim Jones cult in Guyana, the Branch Davidians in Waco (Texas), and the Hale-Bopp Comet cult, it is good to have a healthy skepticism toward people who claim that God has spoken to them. Always ask yourself: Do these revelations correspond to the characteristics of God's voice? Do they contradict Sacred Scripture? Is this something that a compassionate, loving presence would say? Does this revelation challenge us to grow and mature so that we can experience more joy in this life? These kinds of questions must be taken into consideration before we treat any message as divine revelation.

While listening to God's voice, be careful of an aspect of ourselves known as the voice of the ego. The ego is that part of you and me that is insecure, self-seeking, and fearful. Sometimes to protect its own interests, it mimics or pretends that it is the voice of God. Remember in chapter 2 when I talked about my mother who was diagnosed with a tumor in her spinal cord? I felt that God wanted me to take care of her, even to the point of neglecting my health and my need for relaxation. However, this was a case when my ego was pretending to speak for God. It caused me to feel guilt for taking one day to relax away from the nursing home. Yet, if I wound up in the hospital from complete exhaustion, I couldn't take care of my mother anyway. The voice of God will never tell you to make sacrifices that will bring destructive outcomes for you and others. God leaves things like making sacrifices up to our free will. At the same time, He guides us through our feelings and intellect to make decisions that will be the best thing for you and everyone else. Be skeptical of a voice that speaks for God and tells you to make sacrifices that will not be good either now or in the long run for you and others.

And yet, you don't want to be overly skeptical to the point where you close yourself off from hearing the voice of God even when He is trying to reach you. This is why it is so important to practice listening to God's voice. If in the beginning you have trouble hearing God's voice, don't get discouraged. As with most things, it takes time and practice; it won't happen overnight. But if you don't do anything else discussed in this book, please, please practice listening to the voice of God. This is one of the most important gifts that you can give yourself. You won't regret it; I guarantee it.

One way to practice listening to the voice of God is to ask yourself this question: What would God say to me at this moment? What would an all-loving presence say to me in this situation? Once you answer this question, then say to yourself whatever God would say to you as if He were speaking to you. Talk to yourself as if God were speaking to you. For example, if you envision God saying to you, "My son or my daughter, spend some time today resting," then say this to yourself as if God were speaking to you. When you say to yourself the things that God would say to you, then you are becoming more attuned to God's voice, His divine energy, the energy of the universe. And in a relatively short time you won't have to ask what would God say because you will hear God speaking to you without effort.

Happiness That Is Guaranteed

When you hear God's compassionate voice coming through during your exercise, you will feel a sense of wholeness, a sense of being loved forever. You will feel this way because it is coming from a *real presence* deep in your soul. It will not be an artificial or perfunctory feeling, like you are pretending to hear these compassionate words. Instead, it will be *real* because you are open to receiving it and because it is happening to you. You are caught up in the current of divine energy and presence, and, for a moment the world will stand still. You may feel a tingling sensation go through you, which is the divine current. Enjoy. Now you are in touch with the life that has always been with you; power like that will cause miracles to happen in your life. Words cannot describe it. But you will know when it is happening to you.

When God expresses Himself to you, He may not always do it with words. A feeling of peace and calmness may come over you, which is His desire for you. Sometimes, you may feel restless, which is often God's invitation to wrestle with Him. At times, our experience of God is born out of our struggle to stop treating things and certain individuals as our God and to stop needing others to validate our existence. We have worth because God created us to be who we are. Therefore, He may not always express Himself in words, but He does communicate life through our existence or presence on the earth.

Sometimes God may ask you to do something that you might not necessarily want to do. While the message is clear, you may not understand why He is asking you to execute a particular act. If you do not understand what He is saying, tell Him and then listen. His message will become clearer to you if you do not give up trying to understand. For instance, a few months ago God asked me

Gregory F. Bearstop

to forgive a friend who did not seem intent on reimbursing the money he borrowed. There have been three or four occasions in a span of two years when I asked him for the money. Each time, he said that he was lacking in funds, and then he insisted that he would pay back the money; however, a month later, he bought a new car. Now you can see why I have difficulty forgiving this person! I told God about the anger, doubt, and hurt that I was feeling. I also consulted my friends to help me understand God's request. As I began to talk more with God and allow Him to teach me the wisdom that leads to happiness, forgiving my friend became less difficult. Through this ordeal, I learned that forgiveness helps the person who is angry or hurting just as much as the person who commits wrong. Forgiveness is giving permission to myself to continue to love when I have been wronged. Happiness is not allowing any offense or wrong to snuff out the love, care, and concern I have for myself and others. The power to resist the temptation to snuff out love originates from those few minutes a day spent in God's presence. This is why it is important to respond to God's voice, His presence, even if you do not quite understand what He is saying to you. Usually His message is clear, but we do not know how to implement it in our lives. Sometimes we question why we need to implement it at all. But just as wisdom and insights can be gained when we discuss our problems with our friends, wisdom leading to happiness can be ours if we develop our relationship with God. Therefore, do not be afraid to respond to His voice. Tell Him what you are thinking and feeling. Do not hold anything back from God.

Divulging to God our deepest feelings may take time, as in any relationship; however, you can be sure that He will never misuse this information to do harm. Instead, He

Happiness That Is Guaranteed

guards these delicate feelings with the utmost respect. Even if you are hesitant in speaking with God because you feel that He does not always listen (or for whatever reason), still tell Him why you have reservations. Then ask Him to help you to overcome the obstacles that impede the development of your relationship with Him. Fortunately, our God is a God of freedom. For the most part, outside of being our sustenance for life, He does not force His help upon us. Instead, He waits patiently for us to welcome His help into our lives.

Do not become discouraged if it seems that God has neglected to help you. First, He may have sent help several times, but we refused it because it did not come in the form we wanted. Second, He may want us to use our gifts to take initiative in solving a problem. Third, while pain, suffering, and struggle are a part of this world of time and space, sometimes they can be used to make us stronger and better people. Consider when you were promoted to a higher grade or level in school. It required times of struggling through tests and times when you may have felt discouraged. But through all of this, you gained more knowledge, became wiser, and were promoted to the next level. In these situations, pain and struggle molded and shaped you into a more holistic or well rounded person.

However, when it seems that God has neglected us and does not help us the way we desire, we become frustrated and angry. Often we draw the conclusion that God does not care as much as we thought. Then we find ourselves drifting farther away or becoming distant in our relationship with Him. Yet, we continue to struggle through life's perils, not realizing that our pain and suffering often increase when we move away from God. During times like these, we need to remind ourselves that God, being love itself, by His very nature does not fail us. It is important to remember that we are free, in the sense that no one forces us to acknowledge God, at the same time, God is also free to give the best responds to our needs. This responds may not always be what we planned. On the other hand, sometimes God will surprise us and give us what we ask for and more. But it is the best response to our needs if we knew what He knows. He knows everything. We know only a small portion of that. His actions and decisions are based upon having all knowledge. Our actions and decisions are based upon limited knowledge.

THE FOURTH STEP:

FRIENDSHIP WITH GOD

The fourth step in developing your relationship with God is **establishing a friendship with Him**. To become friends with God means that we begin to develop a mutually caring affectionate relationship with Him. In doing so, there are two important details that we must keep in mind, because without them our friendship is deficient and, in some cases, nonexistent. First, our friendship with God or anyone else ought to be mutual. One person does not do all the giving and rarely receive anything. Likewise, one person does not do all the receiving and rarely give anything; both give and both receive. We cannot give to the infinite extent that God can; however, it is important that we give. At the same time, what is given is just as important. For example, God gives us the sun every day, the dawning of a new day, and, essentially, He gives us life that He sustains. In return, we need to ask ourselves, What are we giving Him? This question leads us to the second element that makes a friendship possible.

Happiness That Is Guaranteed

The second element is action. In friendship, your actions—what you do—are one of the best indications of whether you are a true friend. You and I can say anything to anyone, including God, but eventually actions will tell the truth. Suppose someone told you that she was your friend; yet every time you needed to talk with her, she had no time for you. Hopefully, at some point, you will get the hint that this person is not acting like a friend because a true friend would make some arrangements to set aside time for you. These same dynamics apply to our relationship with God. It is not enough to tell God how much He means to us. We need to *show* Him.

As we mentioned in step two, God is always trying to get our attention. He captivates us with the blossoms in spring. He warms us with experiences of falling in love. He encourages us to tell Him about our problems and our achievements. He listens to us even when we feel that He has neglected us. He speaks to us, and we hear His voice when we tune out other voices that distract us. These actions are God's way of showing His concern for us. By showing concern for us, He invites us to be friends with Him.

Think back to how you became friends with the people who are dear to you. At some point, they reached out to you and did something that showed their concern for you. As these acts of kindness occurred and as you felt cared about, you were faced with making a decision to respond to this person's kindness. Because he or she is your friend, you responded to that person by doing acts that also demonstrated your concern for him or her. These are the dynamics that maintain our friendships to this day. Our actions of concern and kindness, more than our words, are the measure of true friendship. Thus it is the same with

God. For the most part, how we treat ourselves and others plays a large role in determining our friendship with God. Also, becoming overly scrupulous about our treatment of self and others is not healthy. No one lives a perfectly charitable life. We all do and say things that we regret; however, even on these occasions, all is not lost. We can continue to be a beacon of love by admitting our wrongs, apologizing, and attempting to rectify the damage that we have done. This is why when we do wrong and commit sin, which is our deliberate divergence from love, God encourages us to forgive and make restitution for our wrongdoings. When we try to heal the damage that we have done, we demonstrate that our basic orientation is to care for ourselves and others. It is very difficult to be friends with God if we are abusing ourselves with drugs and alcohol, abusing ourselves in any other way, putting ourselves down, or harming others emotionally by our words and by not caring about their well-being. God's nature is love, and if we are not making love a major, intimate part of our lives, God is not a significant part of our lives. If this is the case, our involvement with God is like acknowledging with a nod or a smile a stranger who we have seen several times during our commute to work, yet we never venture to make any further contact. Only it is worse with God because not only are we limiting our contact with Him but we are also distancing ourselves from the source of our happiness. Thus our friendship with God is not determined so much by how many right or wrong things that we do, but by our orientation toward love.

Therefore, in order for us to maintain our friendship with God by continuing to be oriented toward love, it is imperative that we forgive. Forgiveness is the third element that is crucial to every friendship.

Happiness That Is Guaranteed

A few months ago, a former client shared with me his challenge to become oriented toward love. To protect his anonymity, let's call him Keith. He shared a recent dilemma when he found himself struggling to forgive his girlfriend, Linda. They had been in love with each other for three years; in fact, he emphasized that he had never felt as much love for any woman as he did for her.

Keith told me that six months ago, however, he heard from a friend that Linda had slept with one of his friends from the past named David. This news almost devastated him. He talked about how he felt despondent and confused. He also said that Linda reluctantly affirmed that she did sleep with David and that it did not mean anything. She assured Keith that she loved him and that what happened with David is something that she does not want to continue.

For months, Keith continued to feel hurt, though he maintained a close relationship with Linda. They had many good times together; but Keith couldn't overcome the hurt until one day, during a powerful conversation with his psychology professor, he was inspired to make some bold decisions that allowed him to experience the joy of forgiveness.

Keith proceeded to tell me that one day after his psychology class, he was talking with his professor about how he could not overcome his feelings of hurt from Linda's infidelity. His professor asked him a blunt question, "Deep in your heart, what do you want?" Keith replied, "I want to love her." His professor responded, "If you want to love her, then love her." The professor explained further what she meant by this statement. As they discussed the significance of loving Linda even after she had hurt him, Keith began to get a clearer picture of what it really meant to forgive and to love another.

Gregory F. Bearstop

Keith relayed to me in an excited tone of voice that he needed to love Linda because this is what he wanted deep in his heart. The problem was that while he was trying to love her, he was actually creating distance between them by holding onto the hurt, anger, and resentment that he felt. He was afraid of being severely hurt again. However, he started to understand that while fear of being hurt can help protect us from future hurt, it can also enslave us and paralyze us from loving others. When we love others on the condition that they will behave in the way that we would like them to, we open ourselves to be hurt. Rather than do this, we keep people at bay, and we limit our care and concern for them.

If we are afraid of losing a relationship with our significant other—because this will also hurt us—we become a slave to the other person's emotions. When he or she is happy, we are happy; when he or she is sad, we are sad. Also, we tiptoe around the person because we do not want to make him or her angry or upset the relatively peaceful balance in our relationship. Therefore, our behavior is dictated by what the other person thinks or feels. To some degree, all of us are affected in some way by what others do; however, when other people's actions begin to enslave, paralyze, and prevent us from acting and thinking in ways that are life giving, then we live a life of slavery. Each day, we, like Keith, are tormented by hurt, unhealthy guilt, and other painful emotions until we are finally freed by the power of forgiveness and enduring love.

Keith told me that he experienced and survived the worse thing that could happen, which was to find out that Linda had been intimate with another man. In his mind, there was nothing else she could do to him. But because he

Happiness That Is Guaranteed

wanted to be free of his pain and hurt, he decided to take his professor's advice. He decided to do what he wanted, which was to love Linda despite her infidelity. She was awestruck by the unconditional concern that Keith showed her. This does not mean that he should continue to place trust in her if she is untrustworthy, but it means that he is no longer controlled and enslaved by the things she says and does. He has decided to love her no matter what happens. If she does not speak to him for several days, he will still remain charitable toward her. This is freedom in the heart.

If we don't forgive, we cannot maintain our friendship with others and with God. We prevent ourselves from experiencing the love, joy, and good times that God gives us through other people. We prevent ourselves from experiencing God, who is in others and who sometimes communicates with us through others. We all make mistakes, do wrong, and commit sin. This is why we need to forgive. In our forgiveness, we are set free from our own pain and hurt, and others are set free to become better lovers. We are set free from our pain and hurt because we are no longer controlled and enslaved by what others say and do. We continue to love and experience joy and freedom because we have decided that this is what we want, despite the actions of other people. Other people are set free because they experience God; they experience what it feels like to be loved without limits. Therefore, they are not nervous because they may make a mistake. They are free to be themselves. Having experienced unconditional love, they will want to practice this in their relationships. Recall how Linda was in awe at how Keith could continue to be charitable toward her, despite her infidelity; consequently, she became more of a caring person because she felt the freedom of being loved without limits. When we feel tense around other people or nervous that we may do something they will disapprove of, we usually do hurt others. We do things to make us feel good without caring how it will affect others. We do this to alleviate the feeling of inadequacy that comes from not feeling loved unconditionally. However, when we feel loved unconditionally, we are free to flourish and become our best self. We become a positive influence that encourages others to be free and to develop their skills and personality. Anyone who influences another person to grow and do things that are life giving are friends of God.

Why do I use Keith's experience of forgiveness to talk about God's forgiveness? The reason is that if Keith, a human being, could forgive Linda after doing the ultimate in his mind, how much more does God forgive us? Even in 1981, Pope John Paul II visited his assassin in prison to offer reconciliation. If the Pope can forgive the man who tried to kill him, God can certainly forgive us.

Often we do not allow God to offer us reconciliation. Sometimes we feel that we are too unworthy and insignificant for God to be spending His time and efforts on us. We also feel that He must be tired of incessantly forgiving us for the same wrongs over and over. Subsequently, we give up on the process and on the opportunity to grow closer to God.

We must stop associating God with *our* standards of thinking and acting. We may become tired of having to forgive so often, but God does not. You and I can never wear Him out, because He has no limits. If we find ourselves committing the same wrongs, such as lying, we must find out why we feel a need to lie. If it is a habit, then we need to implement effective strategies for developing

Happiness That Is Guaranteed

new, healthier habits. The reasons and the causes for our wrongdoings always need to be changed if we are going to enjoy a happier life. The slightest effort on our part to change sinful behavior is the first step to receiving God's forgiveness. His forgiveness is always available; sometimes we are not open to receive it. But if we take little steps toward change, we open ourselves to receive it.

Often the biggest obstacle to receiving God's forgiveness is ourselves. Sometimes it is harder to forgive ourselves than another individual. We cannot accept the fact that we make a mistake; we did something wrong. Even more egregious, sometimes we feel that some of the things we have done are so terrible that they can never be forgiven. There is nothing wrong with feeling this way at times. Feelings are neither right nor wrong; they just are. But when we refuse to choose life and to forgive ourselves, no matter how terrible the act, we have a grave problem. Believe it or not, this is arrogance and conceit. It is conceit because sometimes behind refusing to forgive ourselves in some form is the belief that I am so together that I should not have done something so deviant. However, none of us is so perfect that we are exempt from committing some of the most horrific wrongs. We must realize that we can sin, but we can also do so much more good, especially if we forgive ourselves, which means giving ourselves the opportunity to start to change. It helps to remember that we *make* mistakes; we are not the mistakes themselves. One wrong act does not define who you are. We are the sum of all our thoughts and actions. These thoughts and actions can be healthier, more life giving if we, like Keith, learn to forgive, take steps in the direction of changing the old patterns, and love unconditionally.

CHAPTER 9

A LASTING RELATIONSHIP WITH GOD

Developing a lasting relationship with God begins with your own hunger. Surprised? Did you think that I would say something like a lasting relationship with God begins with prayer? Now prayer is a significant part of it. But we can't even pray if we don't have a hunger or desire. Many of us go through the motions of praying, but we are disconnected from it. It's meaningless. Therefore, what do you hunger for? What do you want? Think about that. The problem isn't so much that we have seemingly insatiable desires. The problem is that we really don't understand that at the root of our hunger, the fuel for that hunger is our relentless desire for lasting happiness. That's what we really want. But we keep camouflaging our hunger by feeding it a diet of things that we think will make us happy. I am not saying this to vitiate the beautiful things in the world and the significant people who have profoundly touched our lives. Truly, these special individuals have given, and continue to give us much pleasure and enjoyment, as I am sure we reciprocate. But they cannot satisfy the deepest longing of our hearts, which is to be loved perfectly. Only the one who is perfect, God, can do this. But we are not easily convinced. This is why we must go through a process of disillusionment. This is the process in which we discover that the things and the people who we thought would fulfill many of our expectations and desires are limited and thus unable to give us lasting fulfillment.

The first step in the process of disillusionment is experiencing our own hunger. Every day we want certain things. This is a wonderful thing because without it, we would not give ourselves what we need to live. But quite often, we are not exactly sure what we hunger for. Therefore, we spend a large part of life trying to figure out what we want and how to obtain it. Over time, we begin to recognize certain desires, and we learn how to satisfy them.

In the age in which we are living, much emphasis has been placed on feeding the hunger of our physical body. A day does not go by when you cannot turn on the television and find a program or a talk show that focuses on improving one's health through proper diet and exercise. Many books have been published that inform us about certain foods that can lower our risk of acquiring life-threatening diseases. Therefore, we are becoming better at feeding the hunger of our physical bodies.

We also feed our minds. We have a tremendous desire to know, to obtain knowledge ranging from gossip to recent scientific developments. We even think that a person is odd if he or she is not aware of major events. At the same time, we are developing our minds. Many prominent figures have emerged who have designed techniques for reconditioning our minds to achieve positive results in our lives.

Thus we are getting better at recognizing and feeding the hunger of our body and our mind. But there is another major part of us that also hungers: our spirit. If you recall from chapter V, our spirit is that part of us that you cannot see. Yet because it has no boundaries or limits, it is our most direct channel to God, because She is beyond limits. But how often do we feed our spirit? More important, what do we feed it with? Sometimes, looking at the way we conduct our lives, I really question whether we know what our spirit needs. Everyone's spirit hungers, but, as with a newborn baby, we try to figure out what it wants. This is the beginning of the second stage of the process of disillusionment, which is the search to satisfy the longings of the spirit.

To satisfy the spirit's longings, we need to know what the desire is like. Have you ever experienced the feeling of a hollow space within you where it seems that no matter how you try to fill the emptiness, you never quite fill it? In fact, the hollow space or void still seems to want something more and better each time. When you feel this, you are experiencing the longings of the spirit and the spirit's need to be filled by something boundless. So how do we fill the void? At this point, we engage in a search for an answer.

Some of us try to fill the void of the spirit with material possessions. But if you ever had a car or some other valuable possession stolen, you start to become disillusioned with the idea that material things can fulfill you. You can't even enjoy your possessions. Thieves benefit from all your hard work. Look at the time you spend trying to secure all of your things. It wears you out. You're tired. Besides, your possessions will never fill the void within you, because they are limited. These things will eventually begin to wear out. Their luster diminishes, and they are soon forgotten. Once this happens, even with all your possessions, you will again feel the emptiness within you. Then you will realize that these things cannot fill the void of the spirit, which requires something endless that gives you joy.

Your search goes on. Sometimes out of your need to fill the void, you turn to money; after all, it can keep your attention. But you will soon find out that money has its limits too. First, everyone is out to get as much money from you as possible; this is a never-ending battle. If you manage to earn or acquire a significant amount of money, even this will not fill the void of the spirit. Money can buy goods and services, but it cannot buy something that is immaterial, endless, and capable of providing constant joy; money cannot buy spirit.

I have a friend who knows a man who has three billion dollars. I will not mention his name or his company because I am sure that you will at least recognize the company. My friend recalls this man explaining how he has three billion dollars in the bank, yet he does not feel fulfilled or happy.

In your life, you may notice that money can provide opportunities that you may not otherwise have. The benefits of these opportunities will give you much satisfaction and fond memories. But after the fanfare and excitement have subsided and you become used to your change in status, the feeling of the hollow void will return if you have not fed your spirit.

Out of desperation to rid yourself of the empty feeling, like many of us, you may turn to sex. It is one of the most pleasurable acts that one can engage in. However, the ecstatic pleasure does not go on forever; it too has limits. Even if you try to spice up your sex life with innovative devices and different methods, the pleasure will eventually end. Again, we ask: Is this it? Is there something more? Yet, in time, when you are fired with passion again, you forget the disappointing conclusion of sex that reminds you of the abysmal void that longs to be filled. Your passion runs its course, but not without reiterating its conclusion.

Realize that during the process of discovering the limits of the things of this world, usually you are not aware that you are searching to fill the void in you. So far, you may have tried material possessions, money, sex, and a host of other things. They may have given you satisfaction for a short while, but they still leave you feeling half full, seemingly never to be filled. At this point, you may accept this plight and resolve to live a life made up of short-lived pleasures.

Everyone, even masochists, wants to pursue pleasure in life. If you are not convinced that there is a spiritual presence that can give you lasting fulfillment, you will probably try to fill your life with instant gratification as often as you can. This is where dependencies and addiction are most likely to develop. For instance, out of a need to either avoid pain or pursue pleasure, you may turn to the use of drugs, as many people do. Although drugs and the misuse of alcohol can give you a few moments of pleasure, in time, they will cause you more pain than you bargained for. Once you get sick and tired of giving your hard-earned money to the drug lords, courts, lawyers, jails, drug treatment programs, etc., it may hit you that drugs have limits too. Ultimately, you become a slave because you can't go a week, month, or year without them, even when they are constantly causing painful consequences. Very few things starve and limit the spirit more than dependence on drugs, which is like being in a cage without bars.

Once you become disillusioned with the trap of drugs and alcohol and realize that material possessions, money, sex, and the like do not fulfill the need of the spirit for lasting fulfillment, you are on your way to having a lasting relationship with God. The hint to obtaining it seems to lie in the close relationships that you have acquired along the way.

In our search to fill the loneliness and emptiness within, we seem to find fulfillment in the relationships where we feel valued and loved the most. There is no feeling that embraces our hearts quite the same as the feeling you get when you know without a doubt that a person loves you. Your conversation and interaction with each other are natural and pleasant. Instead of condemning you when you make mistakes, they show forgiveness and guide you in directions that are life giving. You trust that both of you will do whatever you can to preserve the beauty of your relationship. You do this because both of you have invested too much and you are worth it. If you have a relationship like this or one that is moving in this direction, then you may start to feel that the void within you does not seem so vast and empty. This is because the void or hunger of the spirit is receiving what it needs more substantially. When you have a relationship based upon mutual kindness, peace, trust, patience, respect, care and concern, and the like, you feed the spirit. These qualities are spiritual because they are immaterial and unlimited—meaning that there is no limit on how much kindness, trust, patience, etc., can be shown. Just as your material body needs things that are material, such as food, your spirit needs things that are spiritual, such as the qualities previously mentioned.

In our search to fill the void of the spirit, we have found part of the solution in our meaningful relationships; however, it is only part of the solution, because even in satisfying relationships there are limits.

Through periods of change, if a person's care and love remain constant, we experience an underlying peace that comes from being fulfilled. We start to depend upon our significant other to make us happy. For the most part, our relationship is very satisfying. We want to experience as much love as possible. While doing this, often unconsciously we try to monopolize our close companions, even to the point of having them forgo loving themselves and caring for their needs. As a result, they become distant from us as a way for them to meet their needs. This does not mean that they love us any less. They are simply caring for themselves so that they can be energized to give to us. Sometimes we become angry because, while our companions are retreating or being energized, we are left feeling the thirst of unmet needs. Again the void returns until we are reunited with our companion. Meanwhile, what we experience is the limitation of our humanness. No one will always be available to care for someone's every need or desire. We have enough trouble simply trying to take care of our needs, let alone someone else's. Yet, though we experience satisfaction from our relationship, we also experience disillusionment.

In our disillusionment, we feel as though nothing can appease the need of the spirit for lasting fulfillment. We are tempted to settle for whatever enjoyment comes our way and to weather the dry periods. We appreciate the fulfillment that we get out of our significant relationships. We only wish that there were not any limits and that we could always feel the joy of being fulfilled. But we do not realize that we can feel fulfilled more consistently. The problem is that we have overlooked and have underestimated the power of love that makes our relationships fulfilling in the first place. Too often we confine our experience of love to our significant relationships. When our companions are not present to us, we believe that we will feel less love, if any. Our companions are powerful means of love, but they are not the only means. Love goes beyond the scope of our relationships. Love is the energy throughout the universe that brings things together, and it brings people together. It keeps them together in peace and harmony. Another person does not have to be present to experience love. At this

Happiness That Is Guaranteed

moment, there are magnificent lakes surrounded by mountainous wilderness, and there are lush valleys that are peaceful and uninhabited by people. Yet love is there because you cannot have peace without it. When you see a spectacular sunrise over the ocean, hear inspiring music, or read passionate words that send a tingling feeling of warmth throughout your body, you experience love. This is the power that holds the planets in their orbits. This is the power of love itself. It is not working through any medium; it is just there on its own to be enjoyed. This is the fullness of love that we all want. It is not confined to a physical body or form, and thus it has no limits. It does not need to be reenergized in order to give to us because it is joy, pleasure, and energy in itself. It is perfect; it needs nothing. Because it is perfect, it is God. If it were not perfect, it could not be God. Only that which is perfect is God. Therefore, God can give us what we have always wanted: love without limits. Thus, with God, we can finally have fulfillment consistently and have joy that can never be taken away. But how do we connect with God so that we can always feel this joy? This is where our process of disillusionment reaches a climax. It is here that you and I feel that nothing, not even our most significant relationship, can satisfy us consistently. We hit a bottom where we are tired and exhausted of searching for something that will make us happy. But this time, if we are going to find God, we cannot run from the feeling of loneliness, emptiness, the feeling of wanting more. Sit with it, and allow the feeling of emptiness to penetrate your being. You may find yourself scrambling to grab onto things from the past such as material possessions, sex, or money. This is all right. Just think through your experience of these objects until you reach the same conclusion that they cannot provide lasting fulfillment. Again, allow the emptiness or nothingness to penetrate you until it hits you; you feel that you do not want things that will leave you empty or half full. Instead, you want to be filled. At this point, open your mind to the possibility of being filled by whatever there is out there that can fill you. It is important that you ask God, the source of happiness, to fill you. If you do not ask, She will not impose it upon you. When you ask, wanting nothing more than She who fulfills, She guarantees that you will feel tremendous peace and love. I know because this is how it happened to me.

One Sunday afternoon, I found myself alone at home and bored. I wanted to pal around with someone. I called as many friends as I could think of. But no one could spend time with me on such a short notice. My loneliness prevailed. I sat in my living room trying to figure out how to alleviate my boredom. I thought of watching movies, going shopping, dining out, and a host of other activities. But I had no desire for any of it. Finally, I realized that there was no one or anything that I could think of that could satisfy the depth of emptiness I felt. All I knew was that I wanted something more than the same old stuff from the past. I hit bottom. I placed aside everything and surrendered to whatever was out there that was beyond me. I said this simple prayer: "God, help me." A moment later out of nowhere, I was flooded with love and warmth. It felt as though God had come down from heaven and embraced me. I did not know what hit me. It was incredible. I thanked God, for I felt the desert of my loneliness and emptiness turn into a lush paradise. I had so much energy that I called up a neighbor and took her grocery shopping. The funny thing about this was that I hate shopping with a passion; however, there I was shopping and not minding it. I remembered feeling as though I had a little taste of heaven. There was nothing that I wanted. I had everything.

If you have had an experience like this, when the spirit of God lifts you out of depression and loneliness, you stood on the threshold of a lasting relationship with God. While peak experiences with God are empowering, we also need to develop a lasting relationship with God in our daily living. This happens in three ways: (1) disillusionment, (2) listening to God's guidance, and (3) acting upon God's guidance.

After we experience God filling the void within us, sometimes we are lured back to relying on temporary pleasures to fill the void. We go back to relying on material possessions, sex, money, or needing people emotionally for fulfillment. But these things will never fill the void. This is why our disillusionment with temporary pleasures is the key to having a lasting relationship with God. Each time they disappoint us, we return to God more committed. Keep in mind that we need temporary pleasures because they point to God; they remind us that God can fill the void by the fact that they cannot. When you get tired enough of pursuing the things of the world for your happiness, you will release yourself from them. This is scary because when we stop relying on temporary things for fulfillment, we may find ourselves feeling isolated and alone. Since we don't want to go back to our old drugs or other quick fix, we are not sure where to turn. This is the other side of disillusionment: aloneness. There is a big difference between aloneness and loneliness. Loneliness is longing to be with other people. Aloneness is being with oneself. It is experiencing yourself when you stop depending upon people and things outside yourself to make you happy. At first, this is very difficult. Many of us really don't like to be with ourselves. If you did, you would immediately stop depending on a particular man or woman to make you happy. Yet it is in our aloneness that we encounter the second phase of developing a lasting relationship with God, which is listening to God's guidance.

When you turn to God in your aloneness to find fulfillment, She will guide you to discover who you really are. But God can't guide you if you do not listen to how She is directing you. This is why I emphasized in chapter 8 how crucial it is to listen to God's guidance. When you listen to God, you will discover yourself. Who are you? You may discover that you are buried under a whole lot of garbage that's not you. You are not your successes, material possessions, or what others think of you, the labels that other people put on you. But when you let go of your dependencies, all the things that keep you from loving everyone and being happy, you will find the real you. Many of us live dull, predictable lives. We know what to expect each day, but we don't know our potential. We sit on a wealth of talent. Yet, if we listen to God, She will continuously tell us to live our dream until we get up and do something about it. When this happens, we will come alive again. When you live your potential or dream, you have surprises every day. You don't know what to expect. One day you may be working your regular job, and the next day you are on Oprah celebrating a great achievement. You never know what to expect. Life is exciting. Now how does this help you to develop a lasting relationship with God? When you see all of the wonderful opportunities that will come into your life as a result of listening to God's encouragement as your inner voice, you will always want to be in relationship with Him. This brings me to the third way we develop a lasting relationship with God, which is through acting upon God's guidance.

The doing is the key to having a lasting relationship with God. It is in the doing that you experience the power that keeps you in a relationship with God. When you do what God's spirit, your inner power, guides you to do, your life flourishes. Haven't you been in a difficult situation that could have been avoided if you had done what your first inclination or gut instinct told you to do? Your gut instinct is your inner voice, God's guidance. It looks out for your best interest. Even when other people, out of their insecurity and fear, discourage you from pursuing life-giving aspirations, it gives you the strength to go after them anyway. Because it always affirms you, it frees you to do the positive things that excite you and make you feel alive. God's inner guidance frees you to be your authentic self. This is why it is not slavery, another obsession. You don't have to ask every five minutes: Am I following God's guidance? Instead, it is something you naturally do, because you take time out of your busy schedule to talk and listen to God within you. When you do what God's spirit guides you to do on a regular basis, things you only dreamed of will happen. You will feel freer than you have ever felt because you are in relationship with Freedom itself. Who would ever leave a relationship where they felt the freedom to make all their dreams a reality?

CHAPTER 10

THE DIFFERENCE THAT DEVELOPING YOUR RELATIONSHIP WITH GOD WILL MAKE

1. Through the prompting of the spirit, miraculous things will happen.

When you develop your relationship with God, miracles will happen in your life. It is the power that comes out of this relationship that makes miracles possible. When you listen to what God is communicating to you, when you listen to the prompting of the spirit, you open the door for miracles to happen.

I'll never forget an experience I had as a junior in high school; it taught me the significance of listening to the prompting of my spirit. I was attending a high school seminary in Northeast, Pennsylvania. It was the day when we were returning home for the Christmas break. One of the priests was going to drive me and a few other seminarians 90 miles northeast to Buffalo, New York, where we would connect with flights to our respective destinations. I was taking a flight from Buffalo to spend the Christmas holidays with my family in Washington, D.C. Before I left the seminary, a freshman approached me and gave me the telephone number of his father, who lived in Buffalo. He told me that he had a strong feeling that I would need it. This was strange because I did not really know this student at all. Why he would give me, someone he hardly knew, his father's telephone number was beyond me. I took the piece of paper with the number written on it and did not think any more about it.

Happiness That Is Guaranteed

Two weeks later, after the Christmas break, I flew back to Buffalo to discover that the priest, who was supposed to take the students back to the seminary, forgot me. There I was in Buffalo, with no means of getting back to Northeast, Pennsylvania. Then I remembered that a student had given me his father's telephone number in case I needed it. I called his father, who graciously came to the airport and drove me all the way back to the seminary.

You could look at this occurrence as a coincidence, but I could see God's hand working through the father and his son. How does a schoolmate with whom I rarely talked know that I would need his father's telephone number? I suspect that he did not know. He simply followed the prompting of his inner voice, his spirit, the compassion within him that directed him to give me his father's number.

Sometimes miracles happen when you are not aware of the prompting of your spirit; you have simply allowed God to fill your heart with overflowing compassion. Other people don't have to be a certain way, share your opinions, or do anything, and you still feel an overwhelming sense of love for them. This is a powerful state in which many miracles occur.

A good example of the power of love is an incident I experienced with my best friend, Gregory Riley. We have been the best of friends for twenty years. I know that I can count on him. There is a lot of genuine concern between us.

One day when I was visiting him, I noticed that he had a nasty black-and-blue bruise on his forehead. He was not sure how the sore got there. I placed my hand on the bruise. I remember feeling a surge of power like a magnetic field of energy. After I removed my hand, my friend and I began talking. We forgot all about it. About fifteen minutes later, when I was ending my visit, I politely told my friend to take care of his forehead. But to my surprise, the bruise was gone; there was not a trace to be found. To this day, we cannot explain how this happened. However, I am convinced that when I felt the surge of energy, the wound was being healed by the power of the love that has maintained our close friendship for twenty years. I share this true story as a testimony of the invincible power of love.

2. You will love yourself consistently with confidence and self-assurance.

When you are actively developing your relationship with God, you will love yourself consistently. The relationship itself is very affirming to you. When you listen to God, He will tell you that you can, when others say you can't. With God, you don't feel "I can't"; instead, you are directed to those things that are in your best interest. You feel love that will never end. Because of this, you will feel inner strength. You will not fear people who treat you as though they hold your life in their hands. On the job, some authority figures are famous for this. But in your connection with God, you will be able to tell this person that he or she cannot mistreat you. You are not afraid of losing your job for doing what is right, for standing up for yourself. You are not afraid because you know that in a heartbeat, God can bring another job into your life. This is faith. And God, seeing your tremendous faith, will bless you a hundredfold. Therefore, don't be afraid that someone will take something away from you; indeed, they can take nothing away. All is from God. When one thing is stripped away from you, God is there, waiting to prepare the way for something better. So you don't have to be afraid when your plans are thwarted, because with God you can always be confident that things will work out.

When you feel God affirming you, you will want to affirm and love yourself more. You will love yourself, not conceitedly, but in a way that energizes you to care for others. You will want to do nicer things for yourself. Since God loves you, how can you not love yourself more? When you do this, you become free to discover and to express your unique self by trying different things, experimenting. You do this with confidence because you no longer use mishaps and mistakes as a way to debase yourself. Instead, they become a means to make you better. When you lift yourself, you will uplift others.

3. You will have the influence that will improve your life immensely (e.g., better relationships, more success, confidence, financial security, and so much more).

Again, I emphasize that if you do nothing else described in this book, please, please practice listening to the voice of God. Refer to the section in chapter 8 on communication, especially the exercise that helps you recognize God's voice. When your eyes are open to what God is communicating to you, you will have the influence that will improve your life. A major part of communicating with God is listening. This is what prayer is. Carolyn Miller in her book, *Creating Miracles*, points out that the problem in our relationship with God is that we don't listen. She says that for many of us, our prayer is like calling a hotline number and telling the assistant: "I am suicidal. I just lost my job. My spouse is divorcing me. I am homeless." Then we hang up the phone! We call for some help or advice, but then we hang up the phone. We never give the assistant an opportunity to respond to our needs. This is what many of us do to God. We give Him a petition of all the things we need help with, and then we hang up the phone. We never give God an opportunity to help us and to offer guidance. This is why asking God for what we need is only part of prayer. The other part, which is extremely important, is *listening* to God.

When you listen to God, you need to listen to more than a specific voice. I am not saying don't listen for a specific voice, but don't limit the ways that God can speak to you. Therefore, listen to everything. You know when the light goes on in you. You get excited about it.

The voice of God can come through a child, through a baby. A baby could simply say, "I love you, daddy. I love you, mom." And that may hit you, knock you over. It's the voice of God speaking through the child.

Someone was telling me a story about a lady at a family gathering who was upset because her son had died of a fatal disease. She was angry with God. She did not want to have anything to do with God anymore. She began to cry out, "Where was God? Where was God when this happened?" Then a little child came forth and said, "He was in the same place where He was when Jesus died on the cross." Wow! I thought that was a profound statement. Here it came out of the mouth of a little child. Incredible. The voice of God speaks through anyone, through an eight-year-old or an eighty-year-old, a priest or your worst enemy. Therefore, when we are listening to the voice of God, it is important that we listen in the broad sense to life, listen to creation, listen to everything around us. This does not mean that we literally listen to everything. This is impossible. However, it means that we listen to whatever inspires us to improve our lives. It can come in the form of a book, a workshop, or an inspiring conversation with a stranger. These are the forms through which God chooses to speak to us.

When you develop your relationship with God, you will have a glow about you. People will look at you and say to themselves, "There is a person who lives his or her life so that you can tell that he or she needs God." If you live in this way, you will lack for nothing, because God is with you. You will emanate a peace and joy that can never be taken away. Others will marvel at your sense of peace and joy so much that they will want to know you. They will be drawn to you. You will attract many positive influences in your life. People want to be around joyful people, instead of sad people who always worry. Therefore, you will automatically attract positive influences into your life. These people will be happy to share with you their gifts and talents that will enhance and improve your life. They will put you in touch with people who are in positions to offer you better opportunities. This is how successful people remain successful, because they always attract influences in their lives that facilitate their growth and well-being.

4. Now you can truly love people.

There was a drug dealer whom I would occasionally see on my way to work. I kept getting the feeling that he wanted to talk with me. But I couldn't approach him. I couldn't see myself talking with someone whose life style I hated because of how he has contributed to the destruction of many lives. Yet I felt that God was preparing me to have a meaningful conversation with him. God was challenging me to put aside the label "drug dealer," my opinions of him, and all the things that would limit my connecting with him as one human being to another.

One day on my way home from work, it happened. The young man, who dabbled in drugs for a living, approached me and asked, "Are you a minister?" I responded affirmatively. Then he proceeded to talk about his views on ethics and religion. As he did so, I found myself squirming to find some excuse to get away from him. But he kept talking to me. He told me that he may live at a fast pace, but he also has his moments when he goes to the cathedral and lights candles for people in need. As I listened to him, it dawned on me that this was the meaningful conversation for which God had been preparing me.

I heard an inner voice tell me to relax and don't allow any of my opinions, judgments, or anything else come between him and me, a moment of grace. God was using us as a vehicle to help each other grow. I could not believe that a drug dealer was helping me to grow and become a better human being. I felt freer than I had ever been. I knew from that moment on that I could love everyone. I felt more love in my life than I had ever felt. I realized that connecting with another human being goes beyond the labels, beyond my opinions and judgments of that individual. In fact, I don't love anyone until I can go beyond the labels and stop judging him or her. Sure, I still disagree with what the dealer does, but I am not going to limit my freedom and limit myself from loving even the drug dealer. This is how he will start to change. The drug dealer and anyone else who is mislead wants to know that they are loved for who they are. They do not have to do or say anything. They are loved without conditions. This feeling is the seed for change. This is how Jesus could love the prostitutes and tax collectors. They loved him because

Happiness That Is Guaranteed

He did not judge them. He simply loved them purely. This is what people want.

During my conversation with the young man, he became very childlike. God was using me to help him to wrestle with his life-style of dealing drugs and to grow closer to Him. I could sense the tension in him between dealing drugs and God. Yet, God was with us. Before God, he became childlike. Although he was in his 30s, he needed a parental figure, guidance. God used me to be a parent to this 30-year-old child. How do I know this? Our conversation ended when someone called him and he, standing bashfully, mumbled, "I got to go"; he said this like a child who was being summoned to dinner.

5. You will be truly free. That's happiness.

When you are in relationship with God, you are as free as you will ever be. God is the power within you that gives life to your spirit. He can give life to your spirit that has no limits, because He is without limits. If He could not do this, you would not be here right now. And God is not divided, one part over here and another part over there. God is one. Wherever God dwells, there are no limits; because God dwells in you, there are no limits within you. When you are in touch with God and aware of what it means to have God within you, you will feel that you have no limits within you. Therefore, God is freedom itself. Freedom is having no limits. This is why there is no such thing as freedom outside yourself. There is always going to be something you will have to deal with, whether it is sickness, financial problems, or problems on the job. We cannot always control what happens to us. But we can manage how we cope with whatever happens to us. When we are aware that

Gregory F. Bearstop

God is within us, we start to see or realize that we have no limits within us. Who could be limited when they have God within them? And as you start to believe it, you will start to feel that you have no limits within you. So when the problems come, you are not so worried because you have a sense within you that there is hope for finding a solution. Even if there is no immediate solution, the problem or concern does not prevent you from being happy, because now you are not limiting yourself. As Anthony DeMello says in his book *Awareness*, "You drop the conditions that you are holding onto." Fill in the blank to this statement: Until _____ happens, I won't be happy. Whatever you wrote in the blank is your condition that you are holding onto that prevents more joy from coming into your life. This is how you are not free. For example, consider this statement: My supervisor gets on my nerves. See the condition there? When my supervisor changes his or her attitude, then I will be happy. Until this happens, many days, weeks, months at work will be ruined or miserable. Stop trying to change other people in order for you to be happy. You can't change other people. You are the one who needs to change. You can do this by altering your attitude and outlook on the situation. Let other people rant and rave, and at the same time, you can keep your peaceful disposition if you want to. You can tell them, "When you can speak to me without yelling and with respect, I will talk to you." Then, walk away. Sure, there are times when you will want to respond to someone in a firmer, emphatic tone of voice. Fine. But my point is that your day or week does not have to be ruined ever again because you are waiting for someone to change his or her behavior or because you are waiting for some event to happen in order for you to be happy. Happiness is your decision not to allow anything to

Happiness That Is Guaranteed

limit the joy and fulfillment that you can have daily. When you let go of your beliefs that stifle and control you, then you will begin to feel free. When you feel free, you experience God. We need to get away from this idea of God as the one who tells me all the things I can't do. Whether you are conscious of it or not, God is the freedom you feel. See, you are growing closer to God and didn't know it. The more you become aware of God as the power within you that allows you to feel that there is nothing you cannot do, then you will feel free more consistently. I know that some of you are thinking: "Since I am free to do anything, I am also free to sell and use drugs, have sex with as many people as I can, steal, etc." The answer is yes and no: Yes, you are free to do anything, bad or good, but you are not free if you do things that do not promote your general health and well-being. You might as well be a slave. Activities that do not promote your well-being, such as sex with multiple partners, using and dealing drugs, etc., are setting you up for negative consequences that will severely limit your freedom. For instance, if you have sex with as many partners as you can, you are not as free as you could be. You may have awesome sexual episodes, but you are not free because these episodes are short-lived. True freedom is not something you have a few minutes or hours and then it's gone. It is feeling no limits within yourself on a consistent basis without having to dependent on anything outside yourself to get it. A person who is truly free doesn't need to go to bed with multiple partners. The consistent orgasmic feeling of not lacking anything is better than how you would feel if you had slept with a million partners. Sex with a million different partners is sporadic moments of feeling good. Feeling that you lack nothing because you are aware of God's presence within you is a lifetime of uninterrupted ecstasy.

Yet, how can I have a life of uninterrupted ecstasy when bad things happen to me? To help us understand how this happens, I love to use the image of a hurricane. In a hurricane, there may be whirlwinds of 150 mph all around me, yet in the eye of the hurricane, it is always calm and sunny. However, as calm and peaceful as the eye may be, it is all part of the hurricane, a massive, invincible force of nature. Therefore, the hurricane is a great metaphor that can teach us about how to get through life. Life is a hurricane. There is always a whirlwind of things to contend with swirling all around us. A loved one dies, another bill, someone's in the hospital. We are so enthralled with the 150 mph winds created by the impact of our problems that at the center of it all, the eye goes unnoticed. We forget that within us, there is an eye, a place where it is always calm and sunny. Everything is all right there. You know this place. You've been there. Remember when you danced in front of a lot of people and didn't care what they thought? Remember when you laughed at a joke and thoroughly enjoyed it? Remember when you told someone off and were not afraid of telling the truth? The inspiration to do all these things came from the center of yourself, the place where everything is all right, the place where you feel most free. This is where God resides. When you go to this place where you feel most free, you will feel God's protection. You won't want to leave, and you don't have to. As a result, you will live the rest of your life in the eye of the hurricane. This is the key to life. This is happiness. However, just because you live from your center does not mean that you will not experience the rain and wind; it's all a part of life. There will still be occasions when you will feel mournful, angry, frustrated, depressed, and so on. But the difference is that you will feel anger, frustration, depression, and, at the same time, joy. How can you feel depression and joy at the same time? Well, you can feel two opposite feelings simultaneously. For instance, when you graduated from high school or college, you felt joy because you had accomplished a major goal; however, you may have also felt sad because you were leaving close friends whom you might never see again. You see how you can feel two opposite emotions simultaneously? The same thing will happen when you are in relationship with God, who is the eye of the hurricane called life. You will feel mournful, angry, frustrated, depressed, and, on a deeper level, you will feel profound peace and joy. Sure, for a short while, feelings of anger and depression may dominate. But as you focus on God, you don't worry so much about the difficulties because you know that you have everything within you to overcome the situation. You walk around with a sense that everything is going to be all right despite the challenge. Now you are free.

If you would like to contact the author, you can reach him by e-mail at bearstop@erols.com

Printed in the United States
3304